ES · LIVES · LIVES · LIVES ·

MOZART

MOZART
PETER GAY

Weidenfeld & Nicolson
LONDON

First published in Great Britain in 1999
by Weidenfeld & Nicolson

First published in USA in 1999
by Viking/Penguin

A CIP catalogue record for this book is available
from the British Library.

ISBN 0 297 64346 0

Set in Minion

Printed in Great Britain by
Butler & Tanner Ltd, Frome and London

Weidenfeld & Nicolson

The Orion Publishing Group Ltd
Orion House
5 Upper Saint Martin's Lane
London, WC2H 9EA

To Leon Plantinga
in friendship and gratitude

CONTENTS

MOZART

1 THE PRODIGY

THE LIFE OF MOZART is the triumph of genius over preco-
ciousness. A few five- or six-year-olds of his time could
produce pretty variations on a theme or lure coherent tunes
from a harpsichord with its keyboard covered so that they
could not see their hands. But unlike other mid-eighteenth-
century Wunderkinder, Mozart refined his inventions and
his performances into breathtaking beauty and never showed
the slightest sign of fading into ordinary adolescence, a fate
that has always bedeviled prodigies. In the course of a sadly
truncated life – he died on December 5, 1791, at the age of
thirty-five – Mozart claimed a place at the thinly occupied
pantheon of the greatest composers.

Naturally enough, from his childhood on, ardent
admirers turned Mozart into a celebrity whose life was
obscured by legends. Nor have the scholarly efforts of
modern biographers dislodged the images that fond music
lovers like to summon up when they hear his name: Mozart
the willful child unable to outgrow his infantile ways; the
wizard so captivating that no one dared to question his
credentials for a moment; the miracle worker who never

needed to revise a single note in his lightning-quick impromptu inspirations; the exhausted volcano who took the mysterious commission to compose a requiem as a supernatural hint at his own impending demise; the derelict who was buried in a pauper's grave. Not even his name has survived intact: Mozart rarely used the Latinate middle name Amadeus and greatly preferred the French Amadé.

By and large these tenacious caricatures are distortions rather than fabrications; most of them, as we shall discover, contain a kernel of truth. But many music lovers (like other lovers) demand an extraordinary talent to have lived an extraordinary life filled with memorable encounters, dramatic turning points, and dazzling achievements unduplicable, even unimaginable, by lesser beings. But Mozart's life in music is fascinating enough without embroidery; his reputation as a genius is not threatened by mundane truths.

For Mozart *was* a genius, a rank that the most unsentimental biographer cannot deny him. The aged Goethe, who as a young man had heard the seven-year-old boy concertize in Frankfurt, considered him to be "unreachable" in music, on a level with Raphael and Shakespeare in their domains.[1] Goethe defined genius as a "productive power" whose actions "have consequences and lasting life," and he noted that "all the works of Mozart are of this sort."[2] Hence, when his father called young Mozart a "prodigy of nature," he was not simply engaging in salesmanship.[3] Mozart's symphonies and piano concertos, piano and violin sonatas, chamber music and divertimentos, operas, concert arias, and masses reached levels that only a few composers have ever hoped to approach. Joseph Haydn, who could judge other composers with the authority guaranteed by his own achievement, famously told Mozart's father "before God and as an honest man" that his son was "the greatest composer" he knew "either in person or by name."[4] In 1787, when Mozart was thirty-one, Haydn declined an invitation from Prague to write an opera buffa and called attention to the "Great, the inimitable works of Mozart, so *deep* and with such a *musical understanding.*" If men with influence would only recognize his worth, Haydn asserted, "the nations would compete to possess such a jewel within their fortified walls."[5]

Joannes Christostomos Wolfgang Gottlieb Mozart was born in Salzburg on January 27, 1756, the seventh and last child of Leopold and Anna Maria Mozart, née Pertl. Of his siblings, five died in infancy, and only one sister, four years his elder, survived: Maria Anna Walburga Ignatia, called Nannerl. This appalling balance sheet was only too common in Mozart's century, even among the prosperous; Edward Gibbon's father, for one, gave each of his six sons the same first name, Edward, in the expectation – justified, it turned out – that only one of them would carry it to adulthood.

Mozart's father, Leopold, who loomed large in his son's life, was a well-educated professional musician in the employ of the prince-archbishop of Salzburg as a violinist and assistant conductor – a kapellmeister. His textbook of 1756 on the art of violin playing spread his name across Europe. "The most excellent violinists that Germany possessed in the second half of the eighteenth century," noted one contemporary observer, "were trained by its means."[6] This was the time for authoritative treatises on performance. Just four years earlier, the German flautist Johann Joachim Quantz had published an influential textbook on the transverse flute. If Leopold Mozart had written his autobiography, though, he would certainly have made much of his talent as a fertile and versatile composer. His compositions ran to the playful, but he could turn out a mass or an oratorio, a symphony or a concerto on demand. A few contemporary writers on music bestowed on him the epithet "famous," but only a handful among his works have survived in the repertory; his humorous six-part program piece, *The Sleigh Ride*, is still performed occasionally. In the end, whatever prestige remains to him rests on having been Mozart's father.

As his copious correspondence attests, Leopold Mozart was a keen-eyed traveler and amateur social historian; his pages-long letters home from London, Munich, Paris, Vienna, Milan, and smaller places in between provide precise, valuable information about populations and customs, prices and the local state of health, the attitudes of the upper echelons toward music – which is to say about the Mozarts' offerings – and amusing anecdotes about incidents vividly observed. Another subject with which he liked to regale his intimate correspondents was his health – he chronicled his aches and pains in rigorous, technical detail as well as the medications he took, not forgetting the exact dosage he found most restorative.

Though a lively correspondent, Leopold Mozart was a stern and self-absorbed schoolmaster. The Irish tenor Michael Kelly, who performed for years in Vienna and sang in Mozart's *Le nozze di Figaro*, remembered him as "a pleasing intelligent little man."[7] But not everyone agreed that he was pleasing. His favorite pupils – his children – found him an exigent if professional teacher. "You know," he wrote to a friend in 1766, when Nannerl was fourteen and Mozart ten, "my children are used to working."[8] He tried to control his children's musical labors even when he was on tour with his son. Early in 1770, writing from Milan, he asked his wife anxiously: "Is Nannerl diligently playing the piano?"[9] The portraits of him that have survived suggest a man severe and unyielding, marked by a prominent nose that was the most visible legacy he left to Nannerl and Wolfgang. His invisible legacy was more complicated.

Mozart's mother complemented, certainly did nothing to resist, her husband's ambitions for his children, though on occasion she softened his extreme demands on Nannerl and Wolfgangerl. She had brought no dowry into the marriage, a state that Leopold Mozart a little drily described as "the Order of Mended Trousers."[10] But she compensated for her poverty by being less tense about life, less filled with worries and hatreds than her husband. A sturdy traveler who accompanied her family on several extensive concert tours, she was good-natured, a welcome contrast to her husband's almost paranoid misanthropy; fortunately, considering her family, she seems to have been fond of music. But her paramount duty, as she never failed to impress on her children, was to serve her husband. To her mind, his moods deserved the closest attention; his demands were by definition reasonable.

In Mozart's day, Salzburg, the town and the surroundings that bore its name, boasted some seventeen thousand inhabitants, a sizable city for the time. A small, semi-independent country squeezed between Bavaria on the west and the Hapsburg domains on the east, like most of central Europe part of the decaying Roman Empire, it was mainly susceptible to pressures from Vienna, and largely conducted its affairs as though it were Austrian territory. For many centuries, it had been ruled by a prince-archbishop, who dominated finances, education, the relations of church and state, with the submissive support of a mayor and a town council. The prince-archbishop, too, was the fount of whatever music or theater or festivals the local citizenry might enjoy.

In the course of the eighteenth century, as travelers seeking the wilder, most picturesque aspects of nature discovered, Salzburg was an admirable place for the views. Situated on the river Salzach and virtually surrounded by hills, the town in which Mozart grew up was also amply supplied with colorful private houses and impressive public buildings – the cathedral, churches, the university – mainly dating from the seventeenth century. The urban scenery reminded visitors of a late-Renaissance town; to Mozart, the Italian cities he visited must have looked quite familiar.

Salzburg was a mercantile town; its business was business. Among its inhabitants, only heads of households with a solid occupation – bankers, importers, wholesalers, manufacturers of spices and cloth – were recognized as citizens; during Mozart's lifetime, just around five hundred families, about one in seven or eight, qualified as *Bürger*. This gave them the right to stand for office, and they virtually monopolized the town's government.

But this distinctive legal definition of *Bürger* was at least partially subverted by men of talent and adroitness, especially by those musically gifted, since the love of music was a widespread and authentic passion. The Mozarts were not *Bürger,* but they mixed with them socially, usually on a footing of equality. One of Leopold Mozart's closest friends and favorite correspondents was Johann Lorenz Hagenauer, a leading, prosperous dealer in spices who was also his banker, financial advisor, and, for years, the Mozarts' landlord. Except for passages marked "for you alone," Leopold Mozart's letters to Hagenauer circulated among friends and acquaintances in Salzburg. No wonder that some of the Salzburgers thought that these letters should be published.

As one might expect, the Mozarts thoroughly adopted the values of the local bourgeoisie: hard work, honest dealings, fidelity to one's spouse, prompt discharge of debts. "You know," Leopold Mozart in 1778 warned his son, who, he feared, might incur frivolous financial obligations, "my credit here is good with everybody – as soon as I lose that, my honor is gone," and, he stressed, "you know that honor is more important to me than my life."[11] At the same time, Leopold Mozart, and later his son, led a double life. For in addition to being welcome in Salzburg's leading middle-class circles, they were the more or less humble employees of the prince-archbishop, whose favor or disfavor could virtually dictate the ups and downs of their careers.

An open and affectionate child, Mozart craved affection in turn. He searched for signs of love wherever he could find or produce them. As a six-year-old on a visit to Vienna, his father reported, "Wolferl" jumped into the Hapsburg empress's lap, put his arms around her neck, and earnestly kissed her, apparently hoping for a like response.[12] In the summer of 1763, when he was seven and on a concert tour, he suffered a curious attack of homesickness: "As Wolfgang woke up – I think it was in Augsburg – he started to cry," Leopold Mozart wrote to Hagenauer. "I asked why; he said he was sorry that he did not see Herr Hagenauer, Herr Wenzel, Spizeder, Deibl, Leitgeb, Vogt, Caietan, Nazerl etc., and other good friends."[13] Even though he was with his parents and sister and the subject of flattering attentions, he seems to have felt unanchored and needy. Franz Xaver Niemetschek, Mozart's first biographer, recounts that the little Mozart would keep asking people whether they loved him, and when they playfully denied it, the boy, though given to jokes and pranks, would break down and cry.[14] The inference that he was hungry for more love than he got from his parents is painfully plausible.

Yet it was of course at home that he started on his musical education. When Leopold Mozart took time to initiate the seven-year-old Nannerl in the mysteries of the harpsichord – she was demonstrating a strong talent for it – her three-year-old brother felt inspired to try the instrument on his own. Seeking to secure his daughter's grasp on keyboard technique, Leopold Mozart had compiled a "notebook" of easy tunes arranged in a conventional step-by-step progression, and her little brother soon made the training manual his own. This *Notenbuch* was to acquire historic importance as a source to Mozart's early development. "Wolfgangerl," the father noted with fond precision and unfeigned astonishment, "learned this minuet and trio one day before his fifth birthday in half an hour at half past nine in the evening of January 26, 1761."[15] It had not escaped him that such almost supernatural proficiency was worth immortalizing.

Just after he turned five, Mozart took the inescapable leap – inescapable for him – from performer to creator. Two short pieces for clavier, which his father faithfully jotted down in the notebook, may rank as his first compositions, unless the almost illegible "concerto" he is supposed to have scribbled down a few weeks before deserves primacy. Utterly possessed by music, Mozart had little time or patience for anything else and even wove it into his childish games. And to improve his acquaintance with the muse, he taught himself the violin before he was seven years old. Soon he played it well enough to perform as a soloist in public.

Leopold Mozart did not long hesitate to capitalize on his promising children, and certainly not for their sake alone. They were to be his support in old age. A brief three-week tour to Munich in January 1762 – Mozart was not quite six – served as a rehearsal for more extensive forays to come. Its evident success prompted a longer sojourn in Vienna toward the end of the year, complete with command performances at the imperial court and munificent fees. Even before the Mozarts had spent a month in Vienna, Leopold Mozart could deposit 120 ducats in his Salzburg bank, a sum exceeding two years' salary.[16] Yet these excursions were eclipsed by a grand tour that kept the four Mozarts abroad for more than three years, from June 1763 to November 1766. When the family finally saw Salzburg again, Mozart was ten years old, a seasoned performer and composer.

Much of that tour was consumed with extended stays in important musical centers: five months in Paris, fifteen months in London, and then, on the way back, three months more in Paris, with frequent stops along the way, mainly in the German states and the Netherlands in sizable commercial cities and sleepy capitals of duodecimo dukedoms. The fame of the brother-sister duo had spread across Western

Europe, and they were given ample opportunities for displaying their charm and their precocious musicianship. In city after city, the Mozarts could confidently expect an invitation from the local ruler, from nobles and rich patricians, and assume, for the most part correctly, that one performance would bring calls for others. In London, advertisements for Mozart concerts, at least some of them no doubt written by Leopold Mozart, were addressed to the "Nobility and Gentry." In fact, the touring Mozarts cultivated such exclusive audiences everywhere they went. "We keep company only with aristocrats and other distinguished persons," Leopold Mozart wrote to Hagenauer from Koblenz in September 1763. Uneasily aware that it was inappropriate for him to indulge in such social boasting, he insisted a little defensively that "it's the truth."[17]

Leopold Mozart's travel notes and letters to Salzburg document that it *was* the truth. In Paris, in 1764, the Mozarts dined at the royal table, and the eight-year-old Wolfgang stood by the queen, repeatedly kissed her hands, and had her feed him tidbits. In London, they spent hours with the royal family and became downright friendly with them. "At all courts," Leopold Mozart wrote Hagenauer, "we have been treated with extraordinary politeness, but what we are experiencing here outdoes all the others."[18] Pampered by the great, Leopold Mozart had nothing but contempt for the lower orders; he found them them disgusting and, worse, godless. And he disapproved of the Dutch because he thought them "a little coarse."[19]

Some serious illnesses slowed up the Mozarts during their grand tour; this was still the age of epidemics, and Nannerl, like Wolfgang, caught a touch of all the infectious illnesses going around, including a mild case of smallpox. It is easy to underestimate the perils and sheer inconveniences of such extended tours. Granted, the Mozarts' three-year-long expedition across Western Europe, launched in June 1763, took place under favorable auguries. Their world was again at peace: after seven years of war across Europe, North America, and India, old enemies – France and Britain, Prussia and the Hapsburgs, and the other combatants – had settled their differences. War in the eighteenth century was, of course, less devastating than it has become since. The separation of civilian populations and military forces was still sharp and clear; great cities were not yet home fronts, and the theater and music thrived little less than in peacetime. It is telling that Leopold Mozart fails to mention the Seven Years' War in his voluminous correspondence. But it had severely obstructed travel from one hostile capital to another, and the peace treaties of 1763 removed that handicap. Moving from Paris to London, as the Mozarts did in April 1764, was as easy (except for the seasick-making Channel) as moving from Salzburg to Vienna.

But there were other ordeals quite independent of the international situation. The state of the roads, the hazards of the local food, the constant threat of infection, the unsettling experience of pulling up stakes over and over, the need to learn new languages (in which father and son Mozart excelled), and, in Italy south of Rome, the danger of rampant highwaymen, made these expeditions risky ventures even for travelers as privileged as the Mozarts. There were minor irritations as well: fleas and bugs tormented the travelers. On the occasions when father and son had to share a bed, the son complained of getting little sleep; and in turn the father reported, more in amusement than in anger, that his son snored.

Their succession of triumphs and their lack of enthusiasm for Salzburg kept them postponing their return. The Mozarts had been awash in the applause, often the affection, of the great; from the perspective of the gratifications and the profits they had enjoyed, Salzburg seemed a dim prospect financially, socially, emotionally. It was a place where Leopold Mozart was only a servant, poorly paid and little appreciated.

While each tour necessarily took on the local color, all had much in common. The Mozarts would offer a concert and were rewarded with precious snuffboxes and gold watches or in cash, just as precious to them. They prepared themselves for these events with meticulous care; more than once, Leopold Mozart quite unself-consciously speaks of their "producing themselves."[20] They adroitly flattered those among the mighty they thought truly worth cultivating: the boy Mozart, no doubt at his father's urging, dedicated his earliest compositions to queens, lords, and countesses. This stratagem often paid off, literally. The queen of England, to whom Mozart dedicated six sonatas for harpsichord, gave him a present of fifty guineas.[21] And they dressed as stylishly as seemed befitting the occasion – Goethe still recalled, more than sixty years after Mozart's appearance in Frankfurt, the "little man in his coiffure and sword."[22]

In his letters to his wife, who usually remained in Salzburg, Leopold Mozart retailed such tantalizing details. In England, the Mozarts tactfully adopted local fashions, however eccentric they seemed to their Austrian tastes, and they were astonished at their appearance. From London in

1764, Leopold Mozart exclaimed to Hagenauer: "How do you think my wife and my little girl, and I and the big Wolfgang, look in English clothes!"[23] Mozart's passion for finery dates from this time.

Wherever the Mozarts went, they found that for nearly all their audiences, the habit of listening was at best intermittent. In Mozart's day, music, sacred music alone excepted, was still largely mere entertainment. Its romantic exaltation into a profound semireligious experience that called for rapt silence was still some decades away, though there were signs of it in Mozart's last years. There is a much-reproduced painting of 1766 by Michel Barthélemy Ollivier which shows the ten-year-old Mozart bravely at the keyboard while a select, elegantly garbed assembly help themselves at a lavish buffet table.

The Mozarts tried not to let this casual inattention disturb them. They were hard at work. "Master Mozart" (as London's impresarios called him) was busy performing and quite as busy composing; he cherished the moments he could spare for his life's vocation. Before he was eight, he had written sonatas for the violin, the harpsichord, and other instruments; during the following year, in 1765, he composed his first symphony. It is a lively, distinctly minor work in three movements, the whole lasting some twelve minutes, and scored for an intimate orchestra: four violins and violas, a double bass, a bassoon, two clarinets, and two horns. Like all his other boyish compositions, this first symphony, too, does little to foreshadow his later masterpieces, even though a benevolent listener might detect a touch or two of Mozartian pleasures to come, notably in the relatively individual voices he assigned to each instrument.

The only astonishing element in this precocious effort, then, is the composer's age. It could have been written by someone else, and in large part it was; his father's shadow hangs over it, though we can hardly determine with this composition whether Leopold Mozart acted as copyist, editor, or, far more likely, fellow composer. Mozart spent invaluable hours in these apprentice years listening to the works of composers then in vogue, and like other novices, he diligently copied them out. His uncommonly alert absorptive capacity always awake, he freely appropriated dominant styles, and the musical ideas of his foremost contemporaries reverberated in his own. His manner of educating himself was the manner of nearly every great artist: he struggled toward originality by studying and imitating his elders.

He was fortunate in his youthful journeys to the musical capitals of Europe; they allowed him to hear, at times to meet, the composers he took as his teachers. On his English visit, he made the acquaintance of, and soon became friendly with, Johann Christian Bach, a prolific composer of church music, operas, and symphonies, then settled in London and for some years better known than his father. It was his symphonies that made the greatest impact on the young Mozart; J. C. Bach's Italianate gracefulness, lightheartedness, and brilliant orchestration – it was called the *galant* style – based on sound technique, served him well.

Mozart made his debut in the symphonic genre (quickly followed by several more) at a decisive moment in its history. Its origins go back to the so-called Italian overture, an orchestral piece designed to introduce an opera and conventionally divided into three movements: fast, slow, very fast. Mozart's first symphony, calling for molto allegro, andante, and presto, did not depart from this pattern, though before long he adopted the modern fashion of adding a fourth movement. But the roots of his youthful symphonies in the overture remained undisguised: when he was twelve, he utilized his seventh symphony as an overture for his opera *La finta semplice*. It was not until about 1773, when Mozart was seventeen and had written more than two dozen symphonies, that his true genius as a symphonist emerged. No. 29 in A Major (K. 201), rich in original thematic material, stands out as an arresting move beyond earlier exemplars; it would be at home in the repertory of any modern orchestra.

His audiences found Mozart's virtuosity overwhelming, particularly since he was plainly anything but a mindless circus entertainer but showed himself completely at home in the fundamentals of music. His father repeatedly records how this spectacular boy dazzled audiences with his photographic memory, formidable dexterity at the keyboard, and uncanny gift for weaving variations around a theme. Leopold Mozart treasured the fame his little boy was gathering even in prospect. "Now 4 sonatas by Mr. Wolfgang Mozart are at the engraver's," he wrote from Paris in February 1764, "and imagine the noise these sonatas will make in the world when it says on the title page that they are the work of a child of seven."[24] Mozart was in fact almost a child of eight, but this minor, deliberate discrepancy hardly diminishes his accomplishment.

Mozart's gift for learning new instruments was as uncanny as his playing and his composing. Half a year before his sonatas were being readied for print, his father reported: "The latest news is that, in order to entertain ourselves, we went to the organ, and I explained the pedal to Wolferl. Whereupon he instantly proved himself. He pushed away the stool, and, standing, improvised, treading on the pedal as though he had practiced it for many months. Everyone was covered with astonishment."[25] Harpsichordist, violinist, now organist, all at the age of seven.

Nannerl, too, was a talented performer, and widely praised as a harpsichordist as competent as her brother. Showing a glimmer of psychological insight, Leopold Mozart noted that his daughter played so well that everyone talked about her, and thus she no longer had to suffer from comparisons with his son.[26] She also tried her hand at composing, though only for domestic consumption, and Mozart loyally praised his sister's efforts; he urged her to keep them up, though he could not suppress an undertone of disbelief. "I have been quite astonished that you can compose so beautifully," he wrote to Nannerl from Rome in 1770, acknowledging receipt of a song she had sent him. "In a word, the song is beautiful; keep trying something time and again."[27] Yet Mozart's superiority both as a soloist and as a composer was too palpable to be ignored, a reality with which his sister gradually came to terms.

Precisely because Mozart made so powerful an impression, cultivated music lovers anxious not to be taken in by an impostor expressed doubts about the originality of his extraordinary improvisations and precocious compositions. Their mistrust was endorsed by envious competitors who spread word that Mozart's accomplishments were too improbable to be authentic. Given to bouts of suspicion,

Leopold Mozart is not a wholly trustworthy witness, and his repeated denunciations of the cabals against his son in the Vienna of 1768 have an air – to put it mildly – of extravagance. There is no independent evidence for his claim that Gluck was the chief schemer against his boy. His son's rivals, he charged, refused to attend Mozart's performances, since reports of his wizardry, they claimed, were nothing but palpable lies. Were his appearances not sheer bluff, arranged in advance? Is it not ridiculous to think this child can compose anything? The idea of a twelve-year-old writing an opera!

Occasionally given to observations about contemporary culture, Leopold Mozart diagnosed this incredulity as a symptom of a general epidemic of disbelief: "Nowadays, people ridicule everything that is called a miracle and dispute all miracles. Hence one has to persuade them; and it was a great pleasure and a great victory for me to hear a Voltairian say to me, 'Now for once in my life I have seen a miracle; this is the first!' "[28] Skeptics would soon discover that this was not the last.

The composition in contention among the musical powers in Vienna was Mozart's first full-scale opera, *La finta semplice*, an opera buffa. Though no performance could be arranged in Vienna, it was staged the following year in Salzburg. It is far from distinguished. What *is* notable is that the composer was a prodigy of twelve. And that prodigy, intent on showing his versatility, promptly composed the slight one-acter *Bastien und Bastienne*, a Singspiel – an opera with a German libretto and spoken dialogue – a hint, no more, of greater things to come.

In this atmosphere of distrust, specialists never tired of

putting Mozart to the test. From London in 1764 to Naples in 1770, they investigated his background, watched his hands closely, gave him demanding unpublished scores to play at first sight, asked him at a moment's notice to extemporize songs about the passions or to write a fugue. In Florence in April 1770, the Marchese Ligneville, "the strongest contrapuntist in all Italy," presented him with the most difficult fugues and the most difficult themes to work out, which "Wolfgang played and carried through as one eats a piece of bread."[29] Baffled by what they found, these professional doubters were soon reduced to seeking rational explanations for this marvel Mozart. One of these, the eminent Swiss physician Samuel-Auguste-André-David Tissot, who could boast of his acquaintance with Voltaire, thought he had solved "the puzzle of young Mozart" by speculating on the connections between his "moral" and his "physical" organization. In the company of all the other doubters of good will, Tissot was converted into a true believer in Mozart's genius.

A child prodigy is, by its nature, a self-destroying artifact: what seems literally marvelous in a boy will seem merely talented and perfectly natural in a young man. But by 1772, at sixteen, Mozart no longer needed to display himself as a little wizard; he had matured in the sonata and the symphony, the first kind of music he composed, and now showed his gifts in new domains: opera, the oratorio, and the earliest in a string of superb piano concertos. Most of Mozart's works of the late 1760s and early 1770s were written on the road: he occupied the bulk of his time with an extended visit to Vienna and three trips to Italy, all designed to improve his family's bank balance. The expeditions to Italy expanded the lessons that Leopold Mozart had taught his son, and complemented the grand tours to England and France.

In Italy, Mozart greatly profited from his exposure to new musical experiences and took possession of them. The most enduring dividend was the lessons he took in Bologna with the Italian composer and renowned teacher Padre Giovanni Battista Martini in the difficult science of counterpoint, the manipulation of several melodies played together. Martini – the "idol of the Italians," Leopold Mozart called him, and, a little carelessly, "the famous P. Martino" – was in his mid-sixties when the two met, and he immediately took to the fourteen-year-old.[30] Recognizing that he had a genius before him, he defended him against his detractors and, rightly, thought that the best he could do for him was to put him through a thoroughgoing regimen of counterpoint exercises and of that most formal version of counterpoint, the fugue. The benefits of these tutorials were not immediately apparent in Mozart's work, but a decade and a half later he made counterpoint a central device in his last phase. In short, "Wolfg: is not standing still with his science, but grows from day to day," wrote Leopold Mozart to his wife in April 1770 from Rome, "so that the greatest connoisseurs cannot find enough words to express their admiration."[31] Mozart received most of his musical education abroad.

.   .   .

Mozart's promise had never been a secret, and became increasingly palpable year by year. The only question in his enthusiasts' minds was, Will it last? In 1769, the composer Johann Adolph Hasse, then highly esteemed for his operas and oratorios, wrote a letter of recommendation for Mozart that spoke of him in the most glowing terms: "I have looked at his compositions; they are certainly well done and I have seen nothing in them that smacks of a twelve-year-old boy." (Mozart was actually a year older, but the point remains the same.) "I have no reason to doubt that they are his own. I have tested him in diverse ways and he has done things which for such an age are really incomprehensible; they would be astonishing in an adult." He predicted great things for the young man – with one reservation: "One thing is certain: if his development keeps pace with his age something wonderful will become of him. Though his father must not overindulge him or spoil his nature with the incense of unwarranted praise. That is the only danger I fear."[32]

But the Mozarts had more serious matters to worry about. They undertook these expeditions partly to make money, but partly, too, to secure for Mozart that elusive permanent position his father hoped to find for him. In 1770, Pope Clement XIV awarded him the Order of the Golden Spur, a signal honor, and in the same year the Accademia Filarmonica of Bologna elected him a member, even though at fourteen he was six years younger than its statutes provided for the age of admission. Wherever they went in Italy, father and son associated with royalty, ecclesiastical dignitaries, ambassadors, and rich English commoners on the grand tour. They dressed accordingly. In Naples in the spring of 1770, feeling the heat, they acquired a summer wardrobe: Wolfgang, Leopold Mozart wrote his wife, was wearing a suit in fiery reddish tones, "called in Italy Colore di fuoco," decorated with braids and silver-toned lace, and lined with material in azure. Writing to his sister, Mozart boasted that in their new clothes, he and his father were "as beautiful as angels."[33]

But these spectacular tributes proved to be largely symbolic. Even the opera he composed for Milan on invitation later that year, *Mitridate, rè di Ponto*, which proved a great success with the public and the critics alike, had only ephemeral rewards. Yet in the midst of triumphs and disappointments, Mozart kept composing, at the rapid rate that had become his customary speed, and with increasing sophistication. From the time in 1766 when the Mozarts returned from their grand tour to the end of the third trip to Italy in March 1773, he had written more than twenty symphonies, a clutch of string quartets, three short operas, concert arias for soprano, and sacred compositions.

At this time, now seventeen, Mozart had reached his full height, which was somewhat below average and unduly underscored his youthfulness. He was aware of it: when he wanted to imitate the other tourists and kiss the toe of Saint Peter's statue at Saint Peter's in Rome, he had to be lifted up "because I have the misfortune of being so short."[34] This seems improbable, more a poignant joke than a real incident, but it shows how self-conscious Mozart was about his appearance. The several portraits we have of him, though they differ somewhat from one another as such portraits often do, agree on the fundamentals. What they show is a commonplace, hardly attractive face with a pronounced nose and large, serious eyes. Significantly, this last feature was the one that his admiring friend Niemetschek singled out, his "large, intense eyes," which lit up his plain appearance. This description, confirmed by others, captures Mozart in action as composer and virtuoso, an action that no portrait could fully explore but which lives in his work.

2 THE SON

MOZART WAS A GOOD SON. When he was traveling, he wrote home often and warmly, sometimes adding postscripts to his father's letters, sending his mother ten thousand or even a billion kisses on the hand and cordial embraces to his sister. He assured both that he missed them dreadfully, and he obediently, even joyfully, raised his family's income to unexpected comforts. With touching patience and humility, he warded off his father's harsh, nearly always unjustified accusations for a variety of presumed sins of omission or commission. "Allow me only one request," he wrote him pathetically as late as 1777, when he was almost twenty-two, "that is, not to think so ill of me!"[1] From his youngest days he knew to whom he owed the most: "After God," he is supposed to have said, "comes Papa."

Much of Mozart's conduct was perfectly conventional for his time. In the eighteenth century, as before, a father's legal authority over his children was virtually unlimited, at least until they came of age. But, of course, parental – especially paternal – psychological pressures care nothing for such artificial boundaries. Even after he had grown up,

Mozart preferred docility to defiance, though he was increasingly tempted to rebelliousness. Even if he found self-assertion hard, his compliance became a burden rather than an obligation joyfully met. In 1769, he wrote home: "The reason I write mama is to show that I know my duty."[2] This heavy sense of filial responsibility faded only slowly, never to leave him.

Although Leopold Mozart's patriarchal position, solidly grounded in centuries-long traditions, long went unchallenged, he headed a family rather modern for its time. There is no evidence that he, or for that matter his wife, punished the children much, if at all. They had been trained effectively enough to be strictly self-disciplined and to require little correction. In any event, Leopold Mozart plainly preferred heavy sarcasm to a heavy hand. He was not, he announced to his wife, one of those "doubly strict" men.[3] He participated in companionable talk at home or by mail and would sign himself, genially, "Your old Mzt."

Such advanced views did not make him a domestic democrat: in the company of virtually every other man in his century except for a few radicals like Defoe and Diderot, he took it for granted that the male is the lord of creation. "One shouldn't always write to menfolk," he told Frau Hagenauer in early 1764 with gallant condescension, "but also remember the lovely and pious sex."[4] But when he had occasion to write to his wife, left behind while he and Wolfgangerl were abroad meeting aristocrats and making money, he sent her informative, in no way condescending bulletins, omitting only the most sensitive information about his income. Not that he wanted to keep it secret from his wife, but, almost fanatically averse to having strangers know just how much money he (or, better, his son) was earning, he reserved such revelations for future private conversations. And he did everything in his power to foster his son's career.

Wolfgang Mozart was a good son, but was Leopold Mozart a good father? His impact was so conspicuous and so persistent that no biographer has been able to slight that crucial relationship. He was Mozart's teacher, collaborator, advisor, nurse, secretary, impresario, press agent, and chief claqueur. But the question whether his influence was beneficial or baneful, or an amalgam not easily disentangled, remains a matter for debate two centuries later.

By the time Mozart was five, his father realized that he had the makings of a fortune in his family. We have it on the word of Johann Andreas Schachtner, a professional trumpeter and close friend of the Mozarts, that whenever the boy produced a new instance of his startling musical gifts, as he often did, his father would be moved to tears. Schachtner called them "tears of joy and wonder," but they must also have been tears of gratification at the thought of many ducats flowing into the Mozarts' coffers.[5] When it came to young Wolfgang, Leopold Mozart the proud father and the shrewd entrepreneur were one.

In short, as is only too human, mixed motives governed Leopold Mozart's ways with his son. They were darkened by his irrational financial worries and his need to manage Mozart's every move. Yet his laments also sound a tone of real apprehension that goes beyond manipulative mendacity. And he seems to have harbored an even more hazardous, though never fully articulated, feeling destined to disrupt the concord between father and son: he must have recognized that Mozart had outstripped him as virtuoso and composer alike, and with sovereign ease. Psychoanalysts have paid close attention to a son's conflicting emotions about his father, but a father's conflicting emotions about his son, less well studied, at times loom just as large. Certainly during the four years that the Mozarts would spend in Salzburg after returning from their third trip to Italy in 1773, Leopold Mozart could no longer silence the dismaying suspicion that he was but an assistant to one of the greatest composers who ever lived.

But to imagine father and son engaged in constant rivalry, or the former merely exploiting the latter, is to underestimate Leopold Mozart's capacity for disinterested love. He was, at least consciously, more proud than jealous, as he boasted about Mozart's latest triumphs, almost note by note and with glowing exclamations. Even setting aside all "paternal partisanship," he thought his son a true genius. In 1764, in a characteristic outburst, he wrote Hagenauer: "My little girl is one of the most skillful performers in Europe, even though she is only twelve, and, to put it briefly, my boy as an eight-year-old knows as much as what one expects from a man of forty. In short: whoever does not see or hear it cannot believe it."[6]

In fact, conscientious paternal concern marks Leopold Mozart's conduct early and late. In March 1765, he told Hagenauer from London that he had refused an offer to settle there even though his earnings were spectacular. The Mozarts had taken in "several hundred guineas" in less than a year. Still, "after mature consideration and several sleepless nights," he had decided that he did not want to raise his children "in such a dangerous place, where most people have no religion at all and where we have nothing but bad examples before our eyes."[7] It was a strange rationale, running counter to the precise catalog of churches, chapels, synagogues, orphanages, and free schools for the poor in London he had sent to Hagenauer just four months earlier. Well informed as he liked to think himself, and often was, consistency was not one of his virtues.[8] As a young man, he had been tempted by heresy; but he had sagely retreated from his religious radicalism, began to profess – perhaps to feel – deep devotion, and tried to instill his children with his religiosity.

Leopold Mozart's protective hovering was particularly compulsive, downright intrusive, as he contemplated his son's inevitable erotic maturation. Nothing would be more likely to liberate Mozart from filial submissiveness, hence nothing was more likely to cause Leopold Mozart the severest anxiety, than the thought that his son might fall in love or, even worse, get married and set up a household of his own. When the family was reunited in Salzburg, the boy was seventeen, almost a man. Even in a century in which puberty came later than it does today, Mozart's age almost guaranteed that he would take an interest in gathering sexual experience, however shy he might be. And Mozart was not shy. We do not know how strong that interest was for him during these four years, and to whom it might have been directed; since the family was together during most of this time, they wrote few of those letters that are the biographer's mainstay. All we have in the letters that do exist is Mozart's casual, enigmatic references to Salzburg beauties to whom his sister should convey his compliments.[9]

His letters support the conjecture that, in Mozart, boyish animation, kept alive into adolescence and even beyond, serviceably substituted for sexual exploration. The Mozarts indulged in a good deal of banter, with the son taking the lead. His messages to Nannerl were unbridled explosions of primitive humor. He wrote her letters switching, sometimes in a single sentence, from Italian to German, English, and French, even to Latin; he made dreadful forced puns, sounded a key word innumerable times as a kind of humorous punctuation; he invented words to make nonsense rhymes, sarcastically praised Nannerl's wisdom, wrote alternate lines upside down, and dwelt on intimate bodily functions. In fact, Mozart's preoccupation with the anus and anal products never waned. This does not say a great deal about Mozart, except that he yielded more readily than many others to the regressive pull of early fixations. Nor were all of these idiosyncratic: his mother, too, did not hesitate to make jokes about shitting, and so did his father.

Whether Mozart was jesting or serious, studying Italian or dressing up for a reception, music always came first in his life. The adolescent Mozart kept composing at the rapid rate he had established in the early 1760s, with his first intensity though with a new distinctiveness. He continued to try his hand at operas. In 1770, at fourteen, he composed *Mitridate, rè di Ponto*, an opera seria on commission from Milan, and a year later, as a repeat performance for Milan, he wrote *Lucio Silla*, another opera seria. This genre, whose popularity was beginning to wane, featured highly placed protagonists, heroic action, dignified speech, and, usually, happy endings thanks to the intervention of a gracious ruler, with literally dozens of composers – including Mozart – using libretti by the prolific Italian poet Pietro Metastasio.

Both of these youthful ventures were well received at the time. "God be praised," Leopold Mozart wrote to his wife triumphantly of *Mitridate*, "the first performance of the opera took place on the 26th [of December] to general applause." Two events unprecedented in the Milan opera house, he reported, had taken place that night: though it was against all custom to have the prima donna repeat an aria at a premiere, it had happened now; and after nearly all the arias, there was "an astonishing clapping of hands and calls were heard: Viva il Maestro, viva il Maestrino."[10] Similarly, the little maestro's *Lucio Silla* flourished greatly in the first month, rapidly piling up more than twenty performances despite some unintentional comedy provided by jealous and incompetent singers. The two operas are rarely performed nowadays; but for Mozart they were pointers leading him from apprenticeship to mastery.

By 1773, he was reaching his characteristic voice; it is no longer possible to mistake any of his compositions for anyone else's. Though Mozart's growth as a composer was in many respects gradual, the C-Major symphony, No. 29 (K. 200), already mentioned, signals a quantum leap into maturity. It displays a shift from, though not yet complete abandonment of, the Italian influences that had dominated Mozart's youthful overture-symphonies; instead he turned to the German school, delighting in its more elaborate orchestral textures, expressive freedom, and use of counterpoint. A ready pupil, as usual responsive to new musical experiences, he particularly studied the examples supplied by the brothers Haydn and found the poetic Michael Haydn, though less celebrated than Joseph, especially congenial; he thought a number of Michael Haydn's compositions instructive enough to copy out. Following his freely chosen instructors, Mozart permitted himself, and began beautifully to sound, a deeper emotional note. Though the half dozen symphonies he composed in his four years at home are prologues to the masterpieces he would write a decade later, they are more than promises. They stand on their own.

So do the finest of the five violin concertos he composed in a whirl of inspiration between April and December 1775. They are still a young man's work, but especially the celebrated fifth, the "Turkish" in A Major (K. 219), displays a wealth of invention that is the mark of unfolding genius. "Melody is piled upon melody," the Mozart scholar H. C. Robbins Landon has written of these concertos, "and new ideas succeed one another in blissful insouciance of each other and of any strict formal pattern. What immediately captivates the listener is the matchless elegance of conception and execution, the suavity of orchestration – which even at this comparatively early stage has that natural brilliance which is so characteristic of mature Mozart – and the luxurious delight in pure melody."[11]

Mozart was making quite as much headway in another musical form he had explored before: the E-flat Piano Concerto (K. 271), the ninth, looks forward to its successors rather than back to the charming yet still fairly conventional beginnings. And, inspired by Joseph Haydn, the father of the string quartet, Mozart also invaded that genre, still in its experimental phase, with a rush, composing half a dozen creditable exemplars in rapid succession.

Nor did he stop there: he wrote sonatas, concertos for bassoon and oboe, a number of short masses and concert arias, and another opera, *La finta giardiniera*, more accomplished than its predecessor *La finta semplice*. As the name opera buffa implies, they were, in stark contrast with opera seria, comic operas; and unlike the German Singspiel with its spoken dialogue, they depended on sung recitatives. In a light vein, he composed divertimenti. At the Salzburg court as elsewhere in these decades before the French Revolution, a divertimento was designed to accompany and brighten a joyous occasion, though Mozart endowed his musical diversions with depths that the coronation or the nameday that called it forth rarely lived up to. His appetite for composing was insatiable.

More than once Mozart's father commented on his son's fierce intensity in writing music so many hours a day. Composing, Mozart wrote in the late 1770s, "is my only joy and passion."[12] But the "only" in this sturdy declaration did not always hold true; he found time to play cards or a quick game of billiards and to send his sister impolite jokes. Yet Leopold Mozart's comment on his son's utter concentration was perceptive and just. In 1771, Mozart reported to Nannerl from Milan that "above us is a violinist, below us another one, next to us a singing teacher giving lessons, in the room across from ours there is an oboist. That is amusing to compose by! Gives one lots of ideas."[13] Rather than shutting out his surroundings as he sat at his clavier composing, he enlisted external musical stimuli and made them his own.

· · ·

Sublimation was not enough; eros would not be denied. Composing was all very well, but there were women. And Mozart's carnal needs played directly into the great duel between son and father, who feared nothing more than his son's becoming caught in an emotional, particularly a sexual, attachment. In October 1777 – Mozart was twenty-one by then – accompanied by his mother and stopping in Augsburg on his way to Paris, he renewed acquaintance with a cousin, Maria Anna Thekla Mozart, and was instantly attracted. She responded in kind. Her nickname was Bäsle – little cousin – and she was a year younger than he, scantily educated but spirited, intelligent, full of earthy humor, receptive to his playful obscenities. The two seem to have become lovers within a few days or soon after, apparently initiating Mozart in adult sexual pleasures. His first description of Bäsle, in a letter to his father, was lyrical rather than erotic, a compromise between the emotions he felt and the discretion his father's almost certain displeasure demanded: she is "beautiful, sensible, kind, accomplished and gay."[14] Leopold Mozart smelled danger and sent a sarcastic reply, as though to dampen Mozart's dawning arousal – in vain.[15]

He and his cousin, Mozart told his father, suited one another thoroughly, since both were "a little wicked."[16] This delightful shared affinity drove Mozart's epistolary ebullience, so far practiced on his sister alone, to excesses of uninhibited self-expression. What had been relatively innocent jokes and puns now became frank scatology and no less frank sexuality. Double meanings abounded, and comical repeated phrases or lame rhymes mimicked erotic rhythms. By mid-November 1777, he could write Bäsle, in French: "I kiss your hands, your face, your knees, and your – in short, all you permit me to kiss."[17] No translation can do justice to Mozart's verbal pirouettes; here is a sample from a week before, from the first of his love letters to Bäsle: "You let it out, you expose yourself, you indicate, you inform me, you declare yourself, you hint to me, you notify me, you let me know, you clearly announce that you demand, you crave, you wish, you would like, you want, you command me to send you my portrait, schmortrait. Oui, par ma la foi, I shit on your nose."[18]

Mozart invented new variations on anality, his persistent preoccupation: "Now I wish a good night, shit into your bed until it creaks." Then, "My *ass* burns like fire! What can that mean! – Perhaps *muck* wants out? – yes, yes, *muck, I* know you, see you, and taste you – and – what is this? – is it possible? – Ye gods! – My *ear*, do you deceive me? – No, that's how it is – what a long, sad sound!" Finally, he breaks through to the heart of the matter. In a paragraph playing on what must have been uppermost on his mind, he dares Bäsle to go to bed with him – or, perhaps, to go again. "I ask you, why not? I ask you, dearest clown, why not?" This is what he urgently wants to know. "Why not? – I don't know why not." Indeed, once again, "Why not? – Strange, I wouldn't know why not? – Now, then, you will do me this favor; – why not? – why shouldn't you do it? – why not, strange! why shouldn't I do it to you? – strange! why not? – I wouldn't know why not?"[19] Nor, evidently, did she.

But this exuberant affair remained an episode, though Mozart tried to keep it alive. In order to exclude the outside world, the lovers devised a private vocabulary, in part still undecipherable; had Leopold Mozart known of these letters, they would have corroborated his worst alarms. To Mozart his Bäsle became all in all, at least for some time. "Ma trés chére Niéce! Cousine! fille! Mére, Soeur, et Epouse!" he had saluted her in mid-November 1777.[20] Nothing could have been psychologically more convenient than to have one woman embody his every attachment. But before the new year, though still lusting for his cousin, Mozart had fallen in love with someone else. And, predictably, his father suspected mischief and got deeply involved.

Aloysia Weber, a cool and ambitious sixteen-year-old beauty with a lovely voice, was a daughter of the musician Fridolin Weber in Mannheim, who, having fallen on hard times, earned his keep as a prompter and copyist of scores. Mozart's encounter with the Weber family – there were three other marriageable daughters – prompted agreeable rescue fantasies in him, fantasies of having the power to make a difference in the lives of others. Ominously, to his father's mind, Mozart found the Webers highly compatible, and he mentioned, casually, that he planned to travel with them to give concerts that would restore them to prosperity.

Even though Mozart kept to himself his more drastic newly formed plan to marry Aloysia Weber – "after all, one cannot write everything one thinks," he told his father during this imbroglio – Leopold Mozart, back in Salzburg, was appalled.[21] He sternly reminded his son that the family agenda had foreseen his going to Paris, to "become famous and *make money.*" Worse, he turned on all the spigots of self-pity. Had he not, though "half dead," thought everything through? Was he not a sick man who had packed his son's trunks until two in the morning and then got up four hours later to superintend travel arrangements? Did not the family depend on him, young Wolfgang, for their very survival? "You must with all your soul think of your parents' welfare, otherwise your soul will go to the devil." With every letter, sometimes several times a week, he hounded his son to save money and to earn money – for the family's sake. In February 1778 the thread of his patience, never very sturdy, finally broke. Brooking no contradiction, he turned from suggestions to a command: *"Off with you to Paris!"* And he must take his mother along, even though she had planned to return to Salzburg.[22] As expected, this emotional blackmail worked, and Mozart started for Paris in mid-March, more or less in love with two women, and carrying on his intermittent courtships by mail.

But Mannheim had been not merely an erotic but also a musical revelation. The composers resident in the town had developed a recognizable style of their own – Leopold Mozart called it "the *mannered* Mannheim taste" – famous for its accurate playing, its grace notes, and its crescendos.[23] Its orchestra was the most accomplished Mozart had ever heard, an orchestra extravagantly supported by the elector of the palatinate, Carl Theodor. "The orchestra is good and strong," he told his father. It boasted ten or eleven first and the same number of second violins, four violas, two oboes, two flutes, two clarinets, two horns, four cellos, four bassoons, four double basses, trumpets, and drums. "One could make beautiful music with it."[24]

The half year in Paris stretching from March to September 1778 proved something of a nightmare. The first patron to deflate Mozart's hopes was the duchess of Chabot, to whom he had a letter of introduction. She treated him rudely, took a week before inviting him to her mansion, and when he came to attend her, kept him waiting in an unheated, freezing antechamber. Finally asked to join the company, he found the duchess and a group of guests busy with drawing, and when it came time for him to perform, he was given a "miserable, wretched clavier." And while he played, "Madame and all the gentlemen did not let up drawing for a moment, but kept it up, so that I played for the sofas, the table and the walls." He remembered the first visit he had paid to Paris as a little boy, and concluded that Parisian manners had sadly deteriorated; their much-vaunted politesse now looked much like impudence.[25]

Worse was to come. Contrary to the Mozarts' grandiose expectations, there was little money to be made. Mozart let his father know that he was spending more than he liked in taking conveyances across town, since the "indescribable muck" made the streets virtually impassable. He was giving clavier lessons, an activity he disliked; immersed in music, he told his father, haunted by it every minute, he found that teaching interfered with composing.[26] His mother was bored and unwell. As for the hosts who invited him to perform at their residences, they were lavish with compliments and stingy with fees: "O c'est un Prodige," they would exclaim, "c'est inconcevable, c'est etonnant, and with that addieu."[27] He did find some time to compose, and the Symphony No. 31 in D (K. 297), nicknamed the "Paris" Symphony, was the most important fruit of his Parisian expedition.

The "Paris" Symphony gave Mozart a great deal of pleasure. He had fine instrumentalists at his disposal, many of them musicians from Mannheim, and felt able to score the piece for a larger orchestra than any he had used before. He had come a long way from the small ensembles he had been content with a dozen or so years earlier. Mozart's account of the premiere of this symphony affords an intimate glimpse into his mental processes, the creator's pride in his creation swamped by his apprehension as to just how his offspring would fare with the public. It was performed with great "aplauso" and mentioned in the "Couriere de L'europe." In short, "it has pleased people exceptionally well. During the rehearsal I was really frightened; all my life I have heard nothing worse; you can't imagine how they botched the symphony twice in a row and scratched away at it – I was truly scared." He wanted another rehearsal, but there was no time, and Mozart went to bed with a fearful heart, "in a discontented and angry frame of mind."[28]

In this mood of rage mixed with anxiety, he decided not to attend the concert, then changed his mind, resolved if necessary to grab the first violinist's instrument and conduct the symphony himself. He prayed that things might go well, "since all conduces to God's greatest honor and glory." But "in the midst of the first allegro, which has a passage that I knew would please, the whole audience was in raptures – and there was great applaudissement." To pique his listeners, he had chosen to repeat this passage at the end. "The andante pleased as well, but especially the last allegro." Aware that in Paris concluding allegros usually started with every instrument sounding out, he decided to be original, having the two violins, solo, play piano for eight measures, followed by a forte. "During the *piano*, the audience, as I had expected, went shhh! Then came the *forte*," which brought another wave of applause. To reward himself, Mozart went to the Palais Royale and bought himself a good ice.[29]

Intermittently, Mozart could relay some other good news to Salzburg: in early June, he reported to his father that "the godless and arch-scoundrel Voltaire has kicked the bucket as it were like a dog – like a beast – that is his reward!"[30] But prevailing intelligence from Paris was bad, very bad. Mozart's mother had already been ailing in Mannheim; and in Paris, cold and often lonely, her condition deteriorated. She was suffering from an assortment of ailments ranging from earaches to a sore throat, but her husband, duly informed, was not to be moved; she was not to desert her son in Paris. Early in July she died, and Mozart, playing a curious game of denial, delayed reporting her death to Salzburg, writing of her as very ill when she was already dead. Acknowledging this pious deception a little later, he justified it as a way of preparing his father and sister for the terrible news, but it is probable that fear of reprisals from his father also burdened his mind. In any event, his newly widowed father, who had insisted she go to Paris with Mozart and disregarded her hints that she might be better off at home, promptly blamed his son: he had slighted her, he had refused to take her complaints seriously, he had by his irresponsible behavior in Mannheim compelled her to accompany him to Paris, and he might soon be responsible for his father's death as well! It is a symptom of how securely Leopold Mozart had his son in his grip that Mozart responded with dignity but no visible resentment.

He must, though, have taken offense at his father's scatter-shot and undeserved recriminations, swallowed the replies they deserved, and then, as people with a strong conscience will, turned his anger against himself. "From time to time," he wrote his father in late July 1778, "I have attacks of melancholy." He dealt with them in his accustomed self-starting way: activity.[31] He kept composing and writing letters, among them messages to Aloysia Weber. But she was no longer interested; perhaps she never had been. She had secured a post at the Munich opera, and when Mozart turned up at her house in Mannheim toward the end of 1778, she treated him as though she did not know him. Whereupon, according to Georg Niklaus Nissen (the widowed Constanze Mozart's second husband, and one of Mozart's earliest and best-informed biographers), he sat down at the piano and sang in a loud voice: "The person who doesn't want me can lick my ass."[32] Knowing what we do of him, we may say that the story sounds in character.

There was always Bäsle. His thoughts turned back to her, and on his way to Munich, he asked her to join him there. "If you have as much pleasure in seeing me as I have in seeing you, then come to Munich, to that esteemed town – see that you get to it before the New Year, then I'll take a look at you in front and behind." In short, "be sure to come, otherwise it's a shit; then I shall, in my own high person, compliment you, put a seal on your ass, kiss your hand, shoot off the rear gun, embrace you, clean you behind and in front, pay to the last penny whatever I owe you, and sound out a solid fart, and perhaps let something drop."[33]

Bäsle apparently found this crude invitation irresistible: she came to Munich and then traveled with Mozart to Salzburg. His father did his best to sabotage their reunion – and Leopold Mozart's best was very good – so that Mozart found himself fighting an internal battle between the pressures of his sensuality and the pressures of submissiveness. Once more the good son carried the day. Bäsle did not stay long in Salzburg. And though Mozart and she did not lose contact until about three years later, well before that the old glow was gone.

3 THE SERVANT

AS A SON, Mozart felt the pressure of his father's whims and anxieties; as a musician, he had another master, the prince-archbishop of Salzburg. The first of the two arch-bishops under whom he served was Sigismund, Count of Schrattenbach, who was greatly pleased with having this prodigy in his lands and unstintingly generous to his difficult father. An impassioned lover of music, he commissioned compositions from Mozart and saw to it that they were performed. Perhaps even more agreeable to the Mozarts, he granted them extended leaves of absence for their tours and helped to meet their expenses. To his mind, they were goodwill ambassadors who enhanced Salzburg's reputation wherever they went. But then, in December 1771, Archbishop Sigismund died and was succeeded by Archbishop Hieronymus, Count of Colloredo; and with that, the fortune of the Mozarts in Salzburg, after some initial prosperity, started to decline drastically.

For many centuries, artists – sculptors, painters, poets, playwrights, architects, composers, and performers – had been the servants of power. Historians can point to a mere handful of exceptions. In the early sixteenth century, when Pope Julius II ordered Michelangelo to remain in Rome, the artist could defy his master and leave the city without suffering any consequences, for he seemed somehow more than human to his contemporaries. In the next century, the painters of the Dutch golden age were self-employed craftsmen who often dealt directly with their customers. But the vast majority of artists owed their livelihood to a Maecenas who would commission a comedy or a serenade, and support his talented servants so that in return he might bask in groveling dedications. A number of poets or composers lived on their patrons' estates, underscoring their dependence. Royal houses, aristocratic clans, rich patricians, and clerical dignitaries paid for high culture and set its tone. And normally they got what they wanted.

Then, though most producers of high culture continued to be yoked to their condescending betters, the eighteenth century saw glimmers of a new relationship emerging. It no longer seemed unthinkable for a playwright or a painter to throw himself on the mercies of the market. Early in the century, Alexander Pope profitably distributed his translations of the *Odyssey* and the *Iliad* by subscription, thus circumventing the usual genuflecting appeal to, and need for, a patron. Several decades later, Voltaire, though he never ceased ingratiating himself with monarchs, amassed a respectable fortune selling his epic poem, the *Henriade*, to subscribers (as well as successfully speculating on a grand scale), which secured him the luxury of spreading advanced views from his château while deploying his impressive resources to disavow them. In 1753, in a much-quoted letter to Lord Chesterfield, Samuel Johnson issued a resounding declaration of independence: "Is not a Patron, my Lord, one who looks with unconcern on a man struggling for life in the water, and, when he has reached ground, encumbers him with help?" Two years later, in his *Dictionary of the English Language*, Johnson, his experience with noblemen guiding his pen, famously defined a "patron" as "commonly a wretch who supports with insolence, and is paid with flattery."

Even Joseph Haydn, for decades subject to immensely wealthy Hungarian magnates, the Esterházys, collected the dividends of freedom in Mozart's lifetime. Employed as kapellmeister and housed at the Esterházys' principal palace, Haydn composed on command; he was forbidden to accept a commission from anyone else or publish a composition on his own without his patrons' authorization. In 1790, when the head of the family, Nikolaus Esterházy, died, Haydn got permission to live in Vienna and go on tour. Johann Peter Salomon, a German impresario and first-rate violinist living in England, took advantage of this opening and invited Haydn to London. Haydn happily accepted, paid the city two long visits between 1791 and 1795, and wrote a dozen of his last and greatest symphonies there. Still, after his return to Vienna, he sought out his old patrons, but secured far more agreeable working conditions – his duties were minimal, and he lived in Vienna for most of the year – though he remained nominally in the Esterházys' service until his death in 1809.

Mozart, too, would try to make a living as a freelance composer and performer. But before that break to independence – it did not come until 1781 – he and his father had to swallow the servant's humiliations to the dregs. Their supreme patron at Salzburg, Archbishop Colloredo, was lordly and unpopular, even among his peers: it took forty-nine ballots in the bishops' convocation and considerable pressure from Vienna to elect him.[1] At the same time, even more than his genial predecessor, Colloredo was a music lover and a competent performer. In 1773, in his account of music on the Continent, the English music historian and indefatigable traveler Charles Burney reported that "the archbishop and sovereign of SALTZBURG is very magnificent in his support of music, having usually near a hundred performers, vocal and instrumental, in his service. This prince is himself a *dilettante*, and good performer on the violin; he has lately been at great pains to reform his band, which has been accused of being more remarkable for coarseness and noise, than delicacy and high-finish."[2]

There is a certain irony in the history of the relations between the archbishop and the Mozarts, a history of mounting tensions. In his religious and political attitudes Colloredo was a reformer, an enthusiastic supporter of the Catholic Enlightenment; and to the degree that the Mozarts had any political convictions at all, they were in the archbishop's camp. When he took office, the local economy was in disarray. The reputation of the university had dramatically declined. The court bureaucracy was swollen, notoriously inefficient, and spoiled by privileges it had taken for granted far too long. Colloredo, a diligent and active administrator, ruthlessly reorganized the revenues, at once raising taxes and bringing much-needed cash into the state's coffers. He coolly attacked and drastically reduced his courtiers' perquisites. He drove university students back to their books by curtailing opportunities for idleness and debauchery, appointed a few distinguished professors, and attracted scholars to his minuscule state. What is more, he labored to improve the condition of agriculture by draining swamps. He reduced the application of torture and the brutality of legal penalties. He simplified divine services. If many of his initiatives were at best partial successes, they pointed in a direction the Mozarts could applaud.

To make Colloredo's reign even more attractive to father and son at least initially, the prince-archibshop esteemed the Mozarts enough to give both of them many and varied assignments for his archiepiscopal court, the university, and local churches. Under Colloredo, though not always at his command, Mozart wrote a formidable quantity of concertos, minuets, string quartets, and other music. His compositions never give an appearance of haste, but he was working more rapidly than ever, and composed half a dozen symphonies and the five violin concertos. And in his last five years at Salzburg he was officially attached to the court by holding the undistinguished post of second concertmaster.

It was fitting that in his Colloredo years, Mozart composed an impressive quantity of masses. Eighteenth-century composers indentured to princes, whether clerical or lay, were required to produce church music, often on short notice. Most of these efforts were traditional *missae breves,* serving in a variety of sacred occasions. Mozart was no exception in having to perform this chore, but he took pride in his work in a field that generally suffered from sheer routine, formulaic production, and eminently forgettable compositions. "In this genre," he proudly told his father in 1780, "one could easily compose half a dozen a day."[3] Amid a swamp of mediocrity his masses and sacred sonatas stood out for considerable expressiveness – or the increasingly skillful miming of expressiveness. Mozart's best-known religious composition of these years, the motet "Exsultate, jubilate" (K. 165), dating from 1773, incidentally demonstrates how secular sacred music could sound in Mozart's hands: explicitly written for a famous castrato and the right register for a soprano, the piece has been described as "a miniature vocal concerto in three movements, full of felicitous invention."[4] But whether his "sacred" compositions were at heart pious or profane, Mozart recognized their superiority over the competition. Staying in Munich or, later, living in Vienna, he would repeatedly ask his father to send him the scores of some of his masses; he knew very well that his compositions in that genre would be received with approval.

For all his active life as a composer and performer, Mozart despised his native city; it was, to him, nothing but a backwater and worse. He lamented what he judged to be his desperate servitude in Salzburg – too angry to appreciate that Colloredo had permitted him and his father to be absent from their posts literally for years. Considering the many leaves he had granted the Mozarts, the archbishop, though given to impetuous anger, must have thought of himself as an indulgent master and of the Mozarts as the embodiment of ingratitude. But Leopold Mozart, like his son, saw only his family's grievances and the fleshpots of courts and capitals abroad.

Two issues, intimately related, inevitably doomed the relationship between patron and servants: the Mozarts' increasingly urgent pleas for extended time away from

Salzburg and their all too transparent efforts to find for Mozart what he could not hope to obtain at home – steady, well-paid, agreeable employment. Not that Colloredo gave Mozart too little to do: he was kept busy carrying out official commissions for celebrations at court, for the university, and for local churches. Like his father, who never rose above assistant kapellmeister in Salzburg, he partially subsisted on an ill-paid post, second concertmaster, and had enough free time to eke out his income with composing for local aristocratic and upper-bourgeois patrons. He never ceased agitating for a better post abroad, and his father agitated in his behalf.

When he was away from Salzburg, Mozart was not shy to put himself forward even in the absence of his father. In Munich in September 1777, he openly canvassed his chances for a permanent position with court officials and approached Carl Theodor, as elector of the palatinate, quite directly. Salzburg was a miserable hole, he asserted; its failings loomed all the greater in comparison with the bustling musical scene in Munich, which was only marginally larger than his despised native town. He made no secret of his distaste for his current employment and begged to be liberated from it: "Salzburg," he insisted to his father in 1777, "is no place for me."[5] But his purposeful forays – Mozart also went to Vienna on the same errand – and his pointed letters to possible sponsors in Italy, all of them straightforward or barely concealed job applications, led to nothing.

Or worse than nothing: the Mozarts' unconcealed disdain for Salzburg did not remain a secret to Colloredo and honed his hostility to them. What is more, it gave the imperial court in Vienna, Colloredo's sponsors in Salzburg, every reason to distrust this impertinent father-son team. In March 1777, Leopold Mozart had petitioned the archbishop to grant a leave and was turned down. A little later, a second attempt succeeded, but in an unacceptable form: Colloredo finally gave Mozart permission to travel, but not his father. Unaccommodating as this looks, it is reasonable to read this combativeness as a backhanded tribute to Mozart's genius: Colloredo wanted to keep his brilliant native son at least relatively content.

The Mozarts were not disposed to see it that way. Hence, in August 1777, the archbishop found yet another petition on his desk. This curious amalgam of servility and impudence was addressed, in the standard, almost untranslatable, submissive form, to "Your Highest Princely Worship, Worthiest Prince of the Holy Roman Empire, Most gracious Prince and Lord Lord!" and proceeded to lecture Colloredo: "Parents make an effort to enable their children to procure their own bread, they owe this to foster their own, and the State's, advantage. The more talent children have received from God, the more are they obliged to make use of it to improve their own and their parents' circumstances, assist their parents, and take care of their own advancement and the future. The gospel teaches us thus to earn interest on our talents." This high-toned, patronizing lesson out of the way, the petition, in the best servile style, entreated Colloredo to grant the Mozarts permission to absent themselves from Salzburg beginning in September. And Mozart signed himself his Lord's Lord's "humblest and most obedient Wolfgang Amadé Mozart."[6]

Irritated to have the Scriptures thrown at him, and no doubt noticing Leopold Mozart's fingerprints all over the text that his son had sent as his own, the archbishop dismissed both with curt sarcasm: "Father and son have permission to seek their fortunes elsewhere, in accord with the gospel."[7] Leopold Mozart had overplayed his hand and was compelled to submit a self-abasing petition groveling for reinstatement. He succeeded, only receiving a slap on the wrist for his insubordination. Mozart himself, we know, accompanied by his mother, left for Paris the next month. His lengthy absence could only postpone the inescapable showdown, not avert it.

The duel now shifted to father and son as principal antagonists. For a time Leopold Mozart prevailed, using all the rhetorical devices at his command, a good deal of stick and very little carrot: his son had practically murdered his mother and was doing his best to murder his father; still, his friends in Salzburg were eager to see him again. He wanted Mozart back in his house, precisely where the son did not want to be. Mozart had lived in the great world, and, except for having to stomach a few episodes of aristocratic insolence, had been everyone's favorite. He had consorted with the rich and the titled. In Salzburg, though, he felt mired in the provinces, a subaltern in the archbishop's musical corps. "You know," he wrote to his fatherly friend the abbé Bullinger in August 1778, "how hateful Salzburg is to me." To have the archbishop mistreat him and his father was bad enough; that people in town were making his life miserable was worse. Besides, "there is no theater; no opera!" and competent singers were in short supply. He protested, rather unconvincingly, that he was not insinuating the town was too small for him. Still: "Salzburg is not the place for my talents!"[8]

Leopold Mozart might be his son's chief devotee, but craving to have him in Salzburg to love and manipulate, coupled with the timidity of a once venturesome musician who had come to think a quarter-loaf better than none, overrode his awareness of Mozart's greatness. In mid-September 1778, as he delayed his return from Paris, Mozart beseeched his father to understand: "The only thing – I tell you this straight from the heart – that disgusts me in Salzburg is that one can't have any proper social intercourse with those people – and that the music does not have a better reputation – and – that the archbishop does not believe clever people who have traveled," that is, clever people like himself. "For, I assure you, without travel, at least for people from the arts and sciences, one is a miserable creature! – and I assure you that if the archbishop does not permit me to take a trip every two years, I cannot possibly accept any engagement. A man of mediocre talents always remains mediocre, may he travel or not – but a man of superior talents, which I cannot deny myself to have without being blasphemous, becomes – bad, if he always stays in the same place. If the archbishop would trust me, I would soon make his music famous; that is surely true."[9] And it *was* surely true.

This letter is one of Mozart's most instructive statements about himself; it casts much light on his feeling of self-worth and sense of mission. He had no false modesty about his gifts; since they were God-given, it would be sacrilegious, he thought, to make light of them. And, quite aware of his exceptional endowment, he could argue without self-consciousness that given acceptable working conditions, he might yet put Salzburg on the map. Here was a reasonable son contending with an unreasonable father.

But, as Mozart must have anticipated, the father remained unreasonable. In October, writing from Strasbourg finally on his way home, Mozart made another attempt to state his case, hardly daring to expect Leopold Mozart to recognize its merits. "Only you, dearest father, can sweeten the bitterness of Salzburg for me." When he was in his hometown, he added, he was unsure of his very identity: "In Salzburg I do not know who I am – I am everything – and occasionally nothing – but I don't demand *all that much,* and, at the same time, *all that little* – but just something – if I am only something – in every other place I know it."[10] It was a cry from the heart to which Leopold Mozart chose to be deaf. Mozart managed some further delay, but by mid-January he finally reached Salzburg, with Bäsle in tow, much to his father's disgust. Immediately upon arriving, simply signing a document his father had prepared, he successfully petitioned Colloredo for the post of court organist, a position that paid him 450 florins, three times as much as he had earned as second concertmaster.[11] He was to stay in his new post for two years.

The music that Mozart composed in Salzburg after his return gives no clue to his restlessness and discontent. Much of it, in addition to commissions from Colloredo, he wrote for friends and friendly patrons, and much of it is memorable: the "Posthorn" Serenade in D (K. 320), perhaps the most agreeable of Mozart's many delightful contributions to this genre; the splendid "Coronation" Mass in C (K. 317), with fascinating echoes in later movements from earlier ones and daring shifts in key; and the symphonies Nos. 32, 33, and 34 (K. 318, 319, and 338), in which he continued to refine the symphony as an increasingly expressive instrument for his unique voice. Most extraordinary of all was the Sinfonia Concertante for violin and viola (K. 364), which ranks with the compositions of his final phase, delightful with its spirited conversations between the two solo instruments and of both with the orchestra, and poignant with an andante movement of heartbreaking sweetness.

Then, in the fall of 1780, Mozart was offered an irresistible prospect: to compose once again the kind of music that he always ached to write: an opera. For obvious reasons – the lavish expenditure of resources and the close, prolonged cooperation with librettist, director, singers, and orchestra players – a composer can undertake an opera only once he is commissioned to do so. Carl Theodor, settled with his court at Munich, had the astute idea of inviting Mozart to set *Idomenée*, a *tragédie lyrique* in the courtly tradition of Lully and Rameau by the French composer André Campra. The assignment gave Mozart double pleasure: he was being asked to produce a major opera and, at the same time, to absent himself from Salzburg. If it were not for his father – this became the refrain of Mozart's letters home – he would gladly shake the dust of Salzburg from his boots forever. His hatred – it was nothing less – had grown tightly focused: it was not Salzburg or the Salzburgers that he found growing more intolerable every day but "the Prince – the proud nobility."[12] His father countered by reciting his own ailments in graphic detail and tactlessly speculating (a favorite bludgeon) that had he been in Paris during his wife's illness she would probably still be alive. This calculated thoughtlessness wounded Mozart; but apart from sending off polite protests, he called on work, that proven remedy, to keep his morale from drooping under his father's well-aimed assaults.

Mozart's *Idomeneo, rè di Creta* gratified critics and audiences alike; curious Salzburgers, including Leopold Mozart and Nannerl, troubled to make the trip to Munich for the premiere. What they heard was an opera serious in its libretto, serious in its music. A sacrifice drama in the antique manner, its ambiance is elevated, its pace august.[13] Idomeneo, king of Crete, prevented by a storm from landing at home after wandering the world for years after victory at Troy, vows to sacrifice the first human he meets on shore if the storm abates. The victim is (of course!) his son, Prince Idamante, who loves a Trojan captive, Ilia, King Priam's daughter, a love she silently returns. The fulfillment of their love is threatened by Idomeneo's pledge and by the jealous Elettra, who loves Idamante. Only divine intervention, decreeing that Idomeneo must abdicate and hand over Crete to his son, saves Idamante's life and brings the lovers together. The gods have decided to let the son best the father; one can only speculate whether Mozart found this resolution gratifying.

Idomeneo has always had its admirers. Assessing Mozart's life's work seven years after his death, Franz Niemetschek called the opera an "exalted work" filled to the brim with a "wealth of thought and warmth of sentiment" that speak of the "youthful vigor" one could expect from Mozart alone.[14] Nearly a century later, so expert a musician as Brahms praised *Idomeneo* as being "in general a miracle, and full of freshness, because Mozart at that time was quite young and audacious! What beautiful dissonances, what harmony!"[15] But the majority of operagoers wanted Donizetti, then Verdi or Wagner; if it was to be Mozart, *Le nozze de Figaro* or *Don Giovanni* were more to their taste. It seems as though the stateliness of *Idomeneo*'s arias lost favor in the nineteenth century – to that century's loss.

In the midst of his stay in Munich, an unforeseen event changed the direction of Mozart's life. He had overstayed his leave by several weeks, but the archbishop was in no mood to reprimand his errant servant. He was visiting Vienna in state and, having taken many of his people along, he summoned Mozart to join him; Colloredo was perceptive enough to recognize that this obstinate young man was a gem more brilliant than anything that Vienna had to offer. By mid-March 1781, Mozart had caught up with Colloredo in the capital, to perform for his master. He would never see Salzburg again.

Though cheered to be away from home and surrounded by music, Mozart quickly discovered that giving performances at the behest of the archbishop made Vienna all too much like Salzburg. His first letter to his father, written the day after his arrival, already featured a litany of complaints. Colloredo, basking in Mozart's talents, was making him play for Vienna's high nobility as part of his regular duties and thus kept him from organizing recitals of his own. "The archbishop," Mozart sarcastically summed up the position, "has the goodness to preen himself with his people – robs them of their accomplishment – and pays them nothing for it." He found these command performances unacceptable: "If I get nothing, I shall go to the archbishop and tell him plainly that if he does not want me to earn anything, he should pay me, so that I won't need to live off my capital." Even more disgraceful, Mozart grumbled, at the noon meal he had been seated with the servants, below the valets, who were placed at the head of the table, and close to the cooks and the baker. "At least," he commented caustically, "I have the honor of sitting ahead of the cooks."[16]

Mozart did not say so outright, but one can imagine his thoughts. He was a composer and virtuoso with a Europe-wide reputation who had been fed morsels by a queen, dined with ambassadors, talked music with aristocratic amateurs, felt at home in select society. And now this! A little later he spelled out his indignation: "I did not know that I was a valet!"[17] His rage was more than the private grievance of a class-conscious bourgeois. It was an assertion that a serious musician deserves to rank high on the social scale, an Austrian's counterpart to Samuel Johnson's dismissal of patrons as insolent wretches. Mozart's protests were a contribution to the process of giving the creative individual, no matter what his legal rank, his full due.

Nor did Mozart remain content with mere verbal out-bursts to his father. After weeks of tolerating slights, after having Colloredo calling him gross names to his face – scoundrel, blackguard, rogue, dissipated fellow, and other unarchbishoplike insults – and virtually showing him the door, Mozart resigned from Colloredo's service.[18] The archbishop's irascible temper had subdued his musical judgment.

Mozart knew that his father would vehemently reprimand him for this gesture, but he could stand no more. Trying to win over the being who stood, for him, second only to God, he appealed to his father's self-respect in tandem with fan-tasies of the three Mozarts building a comfortable existence in Vienna. Nothing made any impression on the frightened and infuriated paterfamilias. Cleverly using one of Leopold

Mozart's favorite pronouncements, Mozart virtually copied what his father had preached to him more than once: "My honor comes first with me, and I know that it is the same with you."[19] Actually, he could not be certain that, for all his declamations, his father would place honor ahead of security; he had had ample warnings that his father's view of the world had through the years grown more "realistic," which is to say prudent and materialistic, than his own.

Although the correspondence that ensued over Mozart's resignation held few surprises for him, he found it extremely painful. His father's letters, which came tumbling out every few days, are lost, but one can reconstruct their argumentation through Mozart's replies, which are appeals for support, even compassion, and dignified restatements of his position. "Believe me, best of fathers," he wrote on May 16, "that I needed all manly strength to write you what reason commands – God knows how hard it was for me to leave you; – but if I have to go begging, I no longer want to serve such a master." Three days later, stung once again by a paternal missive, he told his father, gathering strength as the confrontation grew more acrimonious: "I cannot recover from my astonishment, and will never be able to, if you continue to think and write this way; – I must confess to you that I do not recognize my father from a single feature of your letter! – indeed a father, but not the best, the loving father... *my* father!"[20] Evidently, Leopold Mozart had chosen to read his son's rebelliousness as a sign of selfish obstinacy: did Mozart not appear unwilling to sacrifice his personal pleasures for the sake of higher duties – duties to his father?

Early in June, the archbishop's chamberlain, Count Karl

Felix Arco, told Mozart that his father had written him a letter gravely complaining about his son's decision. Though fatigued by Leopold Mozart's unrelenting drumfire – "I am so weary of the whole affair," Mozart wrote, "that I don't want to hear anything more about it" – he almost obsessively returned to the topic that divided him from his father. If you seriously consider my action, he wrote, "it would not occur to any father to be angry with his son about it; rather [he would be angry] if he *had not taken* it."[21] By this time, Count Arco had rudely terminated Mozart's services by kicking him in the rear end. This definitive dismissal has become a standby in the storehouse of legends about Mozart, yet it seems to have actually happened: Mozart himself vouches for it.[22] He paid an exorbitant price for these intense confrontations; during these months, except for several sonatas for piano and violin, he composed nothing. But from now on, Vienna and the dubious blessings of independence were Mozart's lot.

4 THE FREELANCE

IN 1781, WHEN MOZART was twenty-five, and Count Arco booted his behind in that emphatic gesture of dismissal, Vienna was an expanding, increasingly wealthy city of over 80,000 inhabitants clustered within its walls, and about 150,000 more housed beyond, in burgeoning suburbs. The large majority of Viennese lived at the lower edges of subsistence, innocent of luxuries and barely scratching out a meager existence. In its vast gap between the dwellings of the rich and the poor, Vienna was much like other cities, but foreign visitors noted that in this capital the contrasts were particularly egregious. Aristocrats and parvenus built themselves Italianate baroque palaces while the impecunious found shelter in run-down dwellings in dark, crowded, and stinking lanes, and the bourgeoisie, though growing in numbers and affluence, was still relatively small and ranged widely between these extremes.

Still, late-eighteenth-century Vienna had its allure: its music and theater and its rich opportunities for advancement attracted consumers who were affluent or schemed to become so. This part of the city's population provided profits for manufacturers of silk and porcelain and steady employment for laborers in these and related luxury industries. Between 1780 and 1787, the number of publishing houses multiplied more than threefold, from six to twenty-one.[1] And houses specializing in music, notably Mozart's principal publisher, the Artaria firm, which moved from Mainz to Vienna in 1766, flourished mightily. The city's dominant role as the center of government for the sprawling Hapsburg domains made it particularly attractive to ambitious provincials in search of rewarding connections with the powerful. The imperial establishment was an impressively large and impressively influential employer. Mozart never forgot (or his father would never let him forget) that Vienna was the emperor's official residence, and that appointments to coveted posts, including that of kapellmeister, were largely in the emperor's hands. "My principal aim here," Mozart wrote his father from Vienna in March 1781, "is to get to the emperor in some appropriate way, for I am *absolument* resolved that he *shall get to know me.*"[2]

Though only London and Paris outranked it as cities with active musical cultures, Vienna was not yet the mecca of music it would become a few decades later as home to the local master Schubert and host to the German master Beethoven. But in Mozart's day it already relished recitals, concerts, and operas. Emperor Joseph II, until 1780 co-emperor with his mother, Maria Theresa, and then upon her death sole ruler, established two institutions that won him the gratitude of drama lovers and operagoers: a German National Theatre in 1776 and a German Opera two years later. Once Joseph was in full command, the Hapsburg empire, with Vienna taking the lead, leapt into the enlightened eighteenth century. Mozart could not have arrived in Vienna at a more auspicious time.

Even so, the city had no hall devoted solely to concerts; the most desirable venue was the leading court theater, the *Burgtheater*, where several Mozart operas, notably *Die Entführung aus dem Serail* of 1782, had their premieres. It is significant that two Bohemian composers, the eminent Christoph Willibald von Gluck and Carl Ditters von Dittersdorf, whose reputation almost reached that of Gluck, had found Vienna a supportive environment before Mozart settled there.

And Joseph Haydn, though long shabbily treated by Vienna's Society of Musicians, triumphed in the city not through his presence, which was rare, but through his compositions, which far outdistanced in prestige those of all others. Our image of Haydn as the comfortable "Papa Haydn" is a demeaning caricature. Nor was it being prolific that made him exceptional. In his century, most composers wrote easily and incessantly. But, as we have already noted, Haydn was immensely creative. He stands in the history of music as the virtual inventor of the string quartet and the composer who endowed the symphony with a brilliance and dignity it had not known before; late in life, he composed oratorios that continued the grand tradition of Handel.

All this provided Vienna with a heady musical scene from which Mozart could only profit. It was largely underwritten by music-loving aristocrats, many of them creditable performers on their chosen instruments. The richest and most devoted among them, whether from ancient families or recently ennobled, employed house composers and house orchestras, which played for select guests but would have deserved, and pleased, larger audiences. Mozart's most important supporter was Gottfried, Baron van Swieten, an Austrian diplomat and director of the Imperial Library, a thoroughly informed and energetic music lover. As a host organizing private musicales and as governing spirit in the Society of Associated Cavaliers, an exclusive clan of nobles passionate about ancient music, he drew attention in Vienna to Mozart's compositions and provided him with commissions. Van Swieten had been ambassador at Frederick the Great's court in the 1770s, where he encountered the music of Johann Sebastian Bach, a discovery he shared with Mozart as their acquaintance ripened into friendship. It was, for Mozart, a welcome reminder of the long-forgotten lessons in polyphony he had taken from Giovanni Battista Martini in Bologna a decade earlier.

Mozart's reacquaintance with, and new interest in, counterpoint in the 1780s has been called an accident. But it was the kind of accident that happens to the well prepared. Mozart joined van Swieten's coterie soon after his arrival in Vienna. Every Sunday between noon and two o'clock, a small group joined for a private concert in van Swieten's house, and there, Mozart reported to his father, "they play nothing but Händl and Bach."[3] Inevitably it was the Viennese aristocracy – van Swieten's crowd – that became Mozart's most desired audience. In contrast, good bourgeois, many of whom aspired to high culture, proved rocky terrain for his music. He was as alert as any composer to just what his listeners might find irresistible and in giving them what they wanted – within the limits set by his self-respect and the demands of his genius. But his recognition of commercial realities was never quite so crass as his father's, who valued the general concertgoing public far less as appreciative audiences than as potential paying consumers. "I recommend that you not think solely and exclusively about the musical public in your work, but also about the *unmusical public*," he told his son in late 1780. "You know that there are 100 ignoramuses against 10 true connoisseurs – so don't forget the so-called *popular* which also titillates the *long ears*," the donkeys.[4]

But once Mozart reached Vienna in the following year, his father's well-meaning if intrusive advice faded into the background. He had something more absorbing on his mind: he was in love once again. The affair was the kind of coincidence that strict determinists would call destiny. In Vienna, Mozart once again encountered the Weber family, with whom he had first become entangled in Mannheim. Father Weber had died, and in 1780 Mozart's once adored Aloysia had married Johann Joseph Lange, a Shakespearean actor and painter of professional stature. The remaining members of the family – the mother and three daughters – had settled in Vienna, and made a far from secure living by renting rooms in their house. A scarcely suppressed subtext in the Weber family's plans was to find husbands for the sisters, and once he turned up, the Webers must have seen Mozart as a likely candidate for an advantageous match.

Certainly Leopold Mozart thought so. Immediately suspicious, he denounced the Webers' scheme. His son, facing down his father's horrified disapproval, was boarding with the Webers at the time, and even after he moved away he kept in touch with them. He was beginning to take an interest in Constanze Weber. A bitter, undignified war of words erupted instantly. Leopold Mozart's fulminations, an odd mixture of hysterics and realism, arrived from Salzburg with disagreeable regularity: Frau Weber, he let his son know, was a witch intent on trapping artless young men into marrying one of her daughters; Constanze (a reliable source had informed him) was no better than a slut. Reluctantly, Mozart acknowledged that Frau Weber drank too much, though he had never seen her "stewed."[5] And the girls drank nothing but water. Shifting to another front, Leopold Mozart asked his son, did he really imagine that in his unsettled financial position he could afford to marry?[6]

These were characteristic paternal responses even before Mozart declared his intentions. But in December 1781, after months of hints, Mozart decided to be frank: he intended to marry Constanze Weber. "You are appalled at this thought? – But I beg you, dearest, best of fathers, listen to me!" With touching candor, he confessed that "Nature speaks in me as loudly as in anyone, and perhaps louder than in many big, strong lugs. I cannot possibly live like most of the young men today. – First, I have too much religion; secondly, too much love for my fellow beings and too honorable a disposition to seduce an innocent young girl; and thirdly, too much horror and repugnance, dread and fear of diseases, and too much care for my health to scuffle with whores."[7]

That was his medical rationale; he added a convenient pragmatic one, popular among bachelors through the centuries: his temperament was tranquil and domestic, cleanliness and order in his clothing were essential to him, and such requirements made a wife indispensable. In fact taking a wife would actually save money. "To my eyes, a bachelor lives only half a life."[8] Leopold Mozart did not give up easily, and callously appended to his written consent, which reached the happy couple only after the wedding, new fulminations, including dark hints that Mozart owed him money for his expenditures on his son's behalf.

In some measure, the father's campaign, mixing a bulldog's threatening snarl with self-serving and self-pitying demands, was beginning to lose its bite. His son was growing up; he might be wracked by feelings of guilt at defying his father, but he could no longer disregard his own emotional and physical urges. After all, he *was* twenty-five. Constanze Weber, the middle daughter, was six years his junior, like her three sisters a trained musician. Four years earlier he had felt sorry for the Webers' indigence and imagined that he could rescue them; now he earnestly tried to convince his father that Constanze needed to be rescued from her demanding and ungrateful family.

Mozart took care to tell his father that there was more to Constanze Weber than just being a pitiable, patient, and unresentful victim. As though to ward off new blows from Salzburg, he described his bride-to-be as far from beautiful, as though this would make his wish to marry her less obnoxious: "Her whole beauty consists of two little black eyes and a beautiful figure."[9] She is not brilliant, he added, but has common sense, is a sound housekeeper and endowed with the kindest heart in the world. But – and Mozart did not report this to Salzburg – her sensual appetites seem to have matched Mozart's own. True, he did not quite approve of the suggestive freedoms she sometimes took on sociable occasions; in the spring of 1782, half a year before their marriage, the two almost broke off their engagement after Mozart admonished Constanze for allowing a man to measure her calves – part of an audacious parlor game of forfeits – and she was unwilling to tolerate his severe scolding. At the same time, her sociable frivolity must have suggested something smoldering in her that could only have reminded him of earlier uninhibited moments of erotic bliss. She was a tamer version of Bäsle.

Their marriage would be shadowed by tensions but marked also by companionship and sensual satisfaction. For all her frequent visits to spas to restore her health, their life together, both on travels and in bed, seems to have given them considerable if intermittent satisfaction. When they were separated, which rarely happened, he wrote her long loving and concerned letters, telling her he spent half an hour every evening looking at her portrait and assuring her that he longed for her beautiful little ass. Stoutly, a little defensively and apparently not altogether sincerely, he professed that he was unshakably faithful to her even in thought.

Faithful and ardent: in a remarkable late letter from Berlin, dated May 23, 1789, Mozart told his wife how much he wanted her in bed. He even revived the erotic idiom of his youth as if to underscore his longing, and he must have known that Constanze would welcome it. "On Thursday the 28th I travel to Dresden, where I shall spend the night. On June 1, I shall sleep in Prague, and on the 4th – the 4th? – *with my dearest little wife;* – prepare your dear, most beautiful nest daintily, for my little boy indeed deserves it; he has behaved himself very well and wishes for nothing but to possess your most beautiful [. . .]. Just imagine the rascal: as I write this, he sneaks onto the table and looks at me inquiringly. But far from idle I cuff his nose properly . . . now the rogue burns even more furiously and is almost out of control."[10] Here was Mozart writing to what was probably his last love – rumors of several late affairs remain unsubstantiated – in the uninhibited sexual language he had used with his first.

.   .   .

Amid these domestic strains, Mozart was writing music at his customary furious rate. Now he had to work for two, and with the repeated arrival of children – the couple had six, of whom only two survived – for more than that. He composed for a wide-ranging spectrum of audiences: for the court, for aristocrats, for thriving bourgeois, for operagoers as much as for concertgoers, for amateur musicians who clamored for his chamber music, for his most talented pupils. The names of the noble families at whose mansions he performed, to high applause and material rewards, read like a who's who of Vienna's "best" families. No doubt these associations gave Mozart pleasure, but their impact on his income, whether actual or in prospect, loomed large in Mozart's mind. His father had been a ruthless disciplinarian and taxing teacher, and his son had internalized his precepts to perfection.

Indeed, Mozart had taken over enough of his father's pedagogic dictates to turn himself into a shrewd judge of the musical markets open to him in Vienna. What pleased one sector of that market did not necessarily please another, and he made it his business to have something for everyone. Not that he ever wrote trash; he could not have written mediocre music if he tried. Even the one deliberately bad piece he wrote late in life, *A Musical Joke*, a humorous catalog of the worst possible compositional mistakes, was carefully thought out.

In order to gratify so diverse a public, Mozart explored

virtually every possible combination of instruments, delighting in the untried as so many challenges. The chamber music or the concertos that Mozart wrote between 1781 and 1786, the first half of his decade as a freelance composer, exhibit his imaginative daring and his responsiveness to special requests: marches and contredances for an assortment of instruments; concertos for horns; quartets for oboe, violin, viola, and cello; ensembles bringing together horns, clarinets, and voices in varied combinations; an aria for soprano joined by two oboes, two horns, two trumpets, timpani, and strings; trios for piano, violin, and cello, or piano, clarinet, and viola, and much else. He even wrote a concerto for flute, although this was the only instrument that, he confessed, he could not bear.[11]

The all-Mozart concert of March 23, 1783, in which he acted as conductor and soloist in the presence of Emperor Joseph II, gives some idea of his range:

1.   "Haffner" Symphony, No. 35 (K. 385)
2.   Aria "Se il padre perdei," from Idomeneo (K. 366)
3.   Piano Concerto in C, No. 13 (K. 415)
4.   Scena "Misera, dove son?" (K. 369)
5.   Concertante from Serenade in D (K. 320)
6.   Piano Concerto in D, No. 5 (K. 175)
7.   Aria "Parto, m'affretto," from Lucio Silla (K. 135)
8.   Fugue for piano (an improvisation); Variations for piano (K. 455)
9.   Rondo "Mia speranza adorata" (K. 416)
10. Last movement from the "Haffner" Symphony (see number 1)[12]

What makes this program so stunning is not just that Mozart played only his own music that evening, or that he inserted a popular showpiece, an improvisation, to satisfy the taste of his listeners, but that all except numbers 6 and 7 were of recent vintage. His fertility had become almost legendary.

Even this copious catalog gives only the most limited sense of Mozart's scope. He relished working with new instruments like the piano, or discovering new possibilities for familiar ones like the violin. He had been writing sonatas for piano solo and for piano with violin accompaniment from his earliest days as a composer, since his ninth and tenth years. Once settled in Vienna, he refined both genres: after all, the opening gun in his bid for independence from his archbishop was the publication of half a dozen sonatas for piano and violin. In these remarkable compositions Mozart greatly enriched the part of the piano, which still served as accompaniment for most composers, but which, as a contemporary critic pointed out, Mozart gave "equal prominence" with the violin.[13] In the same manner, his piano sonatas of those years display strongly increased dramatic tension, most felicitously in the Sonata in A Minor (K. 310), written in Paris in 1778. A lesser effort, in A (K. 331), concludes with the famous Rondo alla turca. Mozart's work was growing in sheer power, a new expressiveness.

Here, as so often, Mozart attempted to meet his financial needs without betraying his vocation. Some of his most enduring compositions of this period are his piano concertos, written for concerts in which he performed as the soloist. In the five years after his arrival in Vienna in 1781, he wrote fifteen of these concertos, which alone would have

66

made these years impressive, as they pushed the genre to perfections unimagined before. And the six string quartets he dedicated to Haydn in 1785, which rank with his piano concertos, serve as an imposing introduction to his final, unsurpassable period.

There is something appropriate in Mozart celebrating Haydn with string quartets. Just after 1750, when Haydn started composing chamber music, he had at his disposal a few exemplars using the felicitous ensemble of two violinists, one violist, and one cellist. Luigi Boccherini, Haydn's almost exact contemporary, wrote almost a hundred string quartets, most of them resembling each other, not very original and indeed largely predictable. But Haydn made something new of the string quartet; he did for the genre what Caesar Augustus had done for ancient Rome: he found it brick and left it marble.

Haydn's first quartets were still barely distinguishable from music for small orchestra. But by 1770, when Mozart was already an experienced composer adroitly appropriating the best his contemporaries had to offer, Haydn had established the string quartet as a form highly esteemed by amateurs and professionals alike. His contribution to the literature was massive: he wrote well over seventy string quartets, usually in groups of six. A comparison with Mozart's ventures into the genre attests that the string quartets of Haydn's middle period left their mark on the younger man – especially the fine series of the six "Sun" Quartets, opus 20, composed in 1772, which gave new prominence to the cello. "I have learned from Haydn," Mozart is reported to have said, "how to write quartets."[14] If he did say it, he was exaggerating a bit, but not by much.

Mozart's dedication of these six quartets to Haydn seems

effusive today, but its florid rhetoric was customary in his day. In fact, Mozart's admiration for Haydn, here openly proclaimed, was perfectly genuine: just as Haydn esteemed Mozart above all other composers, so Mozart returned the compliment in full. "To my dear Friend Haydn," he wrote in his best Italian, "A Father, having resolved to send his children into the great world, felt obliged to confide them to the protection and guidance of a highly celebrated Man, especially when by good luck he was at the same time his best Friend. – Here then they are, my six children, celebrated Man and dearest Friend!"

Haydn's influence did not manifest itself immediately. Mozart wrote his first quartets in the early 1770s, during his tours of Italy, beginning with a group of seven and then, in early 1773, adding six more. Some of these still gave the viola and the cello little work beyond providing a rhythmic bass line for the "more important" two violins; but there are moments in these apprentice efforts that show Mozart looking ahead to a more balanced treatment of the strings. It was to integrate four equals into a coherent musical conversation, a civilized colloquy, that Mozart accomplished in the quartets he dedicated to Haydn, an innovation he owed only partly to his teacher.

These quartets document his uniqueness as well as anything he ever wrote: the richness, color, and unexpectedness of his harmonies, which at times make the listener shiver; the original turn to his melodies, a power to please and surprise that never deserted him; and the boldness of his counterpoint. Both Mozart and Haydn could be amusing composers – one thinks of Haydn's "Farewell" and "Surprise" Symphonies and Mozart's *Musical Joke* – and both, too, mobilized a subtler wit. But Mozart's particular brilliance reaches heights (or depths) inaccessible even to his beloved Haydn. In 1785, hearing the splendid "alternation among the instruments" in his son's quartets for Haydn, Leopold Mozart experienced a pleasure intense enough to bring tears to his eyes.[15]

For Mozart, "witty" was no synonym for "joyful." Each of his Haydn quartets offers delights of its own, but the last of them, K. 465, is a visit to the darkest regions of his self. Nicknamed the "Dissonance" (one can see why), it spectacularly demonstrates just how expressive Mozart could now dare to be, how willing he was to bend, even set aside, the rules of the game he knew how to play so expertly. The dissonant opening bars in the first movement aroused disputes from the outset, but the rest of the quartet only marginally lightens its nocturnal atmosphere: the dusky, grave tones of the viola and the cello resound prominently throughout.

A small family of anecdotes, not all of them invented, soon grew up around this quartet. It was reported that on first hearing the introductory adagio measures, cultivated listeners blamed a careless printer for permitting a batch of mistakes to escape his vigilance. Others rejected them as simply grotesque, as an aberration in Mozart's oeuvre. Looking ahead two decades, we seem to be catching glimpses of the presumably outlandish innovations with which Beethoven would shock his listeners in the "Razumovsky" Quartets.

By having the bleak dissonances of the adagio preamble to the first movement resist resolution for almost two minutes, Mozart provided chaos with an awesome musical equivalent. The heirs of these agonizing measures, Haydn's prelude to *The Creation* and the introductory passages in the last movement of Beethoven's Ninth Symphony, also depict anarchy. But theirs was the uncreated world, or raw nature in search of order, which Haydn and Beethoven translated into sounds; in Mozart's "Dissonance" Quartet, the chaos virtually explodes from within, as though private tumults, incompletely tamed, had escaped the composer's iron self-control. Not until the statue comes to dine with Don Giovanni to drag him to hell will the listener to Mozart experience similar terror.

With the quartets dedicated to Haydn, Mozart virtually said farewell to the genre, except for the "Hoffmeister," dating from 1786, and the three he quickly put together in the spring of 1791, half a year before his death. This did not mean that he was tired of chamber music; much like other composers of the time, he traveled among the richly assorted possibilities of composing for small ensembles and, down to the last months of his life, sampled virtually all of them. In 1784, he reported from Vienna to his father that there had been a splendid performance of his new quintet for oboe, clarinet, horn, bassoon, and piano: "It received extraordinary applause; – I myself consider it the best thing I have written in all my life; – I wish you could have heard it!"[16] Had Leopold Mozart heard it, he might have wept with pleasure; but not even this would have induced him to forgive his son. The two were by then reduced to occasional and tense correspondence.

After arriving in Vienna, in late 1781, Mozart wrote a German opera, a Singspiel – *Die Entführung aus dem Serail.* Even a claque paid to hiss failed to undermine its immediate appeal. Though performed more rarely than his undisputed masterpieces in the opera literature, it provides pure enjoyment with its long, animated arias, its exoticism, its comic bass and its sopranos. Such as it is, the plot is based on a traditional tale endowed with equally traditional business on stage: it tells of the liberation from Pasha Selim's harem of a captive Spanish lady, Konstanze, by her lover, Belmonte. His plan to abduct her fails, but the pasha, though he discovers that Belmonte is the son of his greatest enemy and covets Konstanze for himself, shows himself a model of chivalry and frees the lovers. As in *Idomeneo*, a father figure leaves the field, this time of his own will.

If proof were needed that Mozart was traveling in select Viennese circles, it was his admission to the Freemasonic order in mid-December 1784. His lodge was called Beneficence, one of the smaller ones among the eight in the city. A vocal admirer of his music, Count Johann Esterházy, in whose mansion Mozart frequently performed, was probably the most prominent Freemason among Mozart's aristocratic friends and patrons. But noble Freemasons – monarchs, prime ministers, landed aristocrats – were, though powerful, in the minority in these lodges; affluent or at least well-connected commoners such as bureaucrats, writers, merchants, and publishers made up the bulk of the membership.

Mozart was put through the mumbo jumbo of the regular initiation rites, which made him an apprentice, then quickly advanced to journeyman, and was almost immediately promoted to master Mason. His reputation as a composer and his assiduity in attending Masonic meetings helped to make his progress both rapid and smooth. He responded to this receptiveness with short Masonic compositions: songs, cantatas, funeral music. One of his greatest creations, *Die Zauberflöte* (of which more later), is steeped in Masonic lore; its oratorical style and its convoluted plot are virtually incomprehensible without some information about this secret society with precious few secrets.

Freemasons, bent on ceremony and pseudo-genealogy, proudly, if quite fancifully, derived the origins of their brotherhood from sources as ancient as they were honorable; but it was only early in the eighteenth century that Masonic lodges began to proliferate across Europe and the British colonies in North America. When Mozart became a member, some seven hundred lodges were scattered across the Western world. They reached Vienna in 1781 with the launching of what would grow into the largest of the city's lodges, True Concord, which by the time Mozart joined the Freemasons had about two hundred members and boasted stars of Vienna's intellectual elite among them. They met and they talked.

With all their commitment to enlightened principles, the Hapsburg domains remained an authoritarian state in which few educated men had enough elbow room to canvass fundamental political and religious issues as a group, let alone put forward plans of reform. Thus Masonic lodges were serious talking shops prompted to acts of philanthropy – coffeehouses on a higher level and with practical consequences. They formed a conspiracy for benevolence. Mozart does not comment on his Masonic convictions, but it is evident that he took considerable pride in his membership. And, taking the lead for once in the perpetual family duel, he successfully enlisted his father among the Freemasons in the spring of 1785.

Unfortunately for Freemasonry, it was doomed to acrimonious internal splits, some of which Mozart had occasion to witness. For all their emphasis on uniformity in ritual practice and the membership's moral aims – there was, to their mind, only a single canon of virtuousness – the lodges were an unstable amalgam of incompatible ideologies. Influential Freemasons indulged in an eclectic mysticism drawn from presumed ancient hermetic sources; at best these votaries of obscure notions uneasily coexisted, but more often they warred, with fellow Masons entirely committed to the moralistic program of the Enlightenment, which drew its energy from critical rationalism alone.

The Freemasons' carefully staged initiation ceremonies, a medley of liturgical mystification eked out with secular sententiousness, offers strong evidence for this mixture. On December 14, 1784, when Mozart and one other novice were inducted, the oration addressed to them began, "Sacred be this day, O humanity! to advance your well-being, two members have attached themselves to the great chain of masons; on the steps of your solemn altar two of your sons have sworn the unbreakable oath that, joined with us, they will devote themselves wholly to virtue and wisdom!" The brothers apostrophized the initiates with grandiloquent rhetorical questions: "What may we not expect from you, my brother, destined to be the teacher of the people, the apostle of truth?"[17] Outside observers wondered whether this stylized performance testified to deep esoteric feelings or merely lent a certain gravity to an agreeable occasion.

Although Mozart was not explicit about the nature of his Masonic commitment, he seems to have sided with the secular Masons intent on religious tolerance and political reform. "A priest," he once wrote to his father during these years, using the disparaging term *Pfaff* for "priest," "is capable of anything."[18] This did not make him into a heretic, but Mozart's Catholicism (like that of his father) was free of bigotry, open to worldly experience, more than a touch anticlerical. We know that Mozart was no Voltairian and, apart from his own advancement, strikingly indifferent to politics. During the last two years of his life, 1789 to 1791, Europe was convulsed by the French Revolution, but there is not a single word in his correspondence about this historic earthquake. But he found it possible to join officials, savants, and philanthropists uneasy with traditional Christian doctrine in behalf of good works and the propagation of wisdom. *Die Zauberflöte*, as we shall see, was many things, but it was also a rationalist Mason's celebration of truth, love, and human worth. As Papageno and Pamina sing in the greatest Singspiel that Mozart composed: "Man and woman, woman and man, reach to touch divinity."

During the early days of Mozart's membership, Austrian Freemasons were enthusiastic partisans of Joseph II, and in return the emperor placed them firmly under his protection. Once Joseph had became sole ruler in 1780, he could move more freely and more rapidly toward reform than he could with his devout mother as coruler. He centralized the administration of his regime. He nationalized the judicial system, forced the courts toward more humane sentencing, and democratized their procedures. He began to reduce the peasants' time-honored burdens. He acted to free trade from its mercantilist shackles. He reduced the powers of the Hapsburg clergy, closed the monasteries of contemplative orders, decreed the toleration of Jews and other religious minorities. As he summed up his program, writing to his brother, who was to succeed him in 1790 as Leopold II: "I have weakened deep-rooted traditions by the introduction of enlightened principles."[19] The partisans of rationalism among the Masons applauded these policies; to them, he was the ideal ruler, a dictator of virtue.

All this approval, however, soon changed into dismay. Joseph imposed his reforms from above with an urgency and pitiless logic that showed little concern for private feelings and private property. He was tactless and uncompromising, demonstrating what the great American historian Richard Hofstadter once called "the ruthlessness of the pure in heart." If he was a scion of the Enlightenment, he belonged to its despotic wing, doing good whether people wanted it or not. And among his victims were the Austrian Freemasons. In 1785, particularly troubled by the assertiveness of their antirationalist wing, unwilling to tolerate a power in the state even semi-independent of him, he interfered with the business of the Viennese Masonic lodges, even the enlightened ones, by compelling them to consolidate into two, appointed new masters to make them responsive to his authority, and strictly limited the number of new recruits. The idea that there is something like a loyal opposition to government was still in the future, and it was first seriously tried in England, not in Austria.

While many Freemasons resigned from their lodges in this time of troubles, Mozart remained steadfast, attracted, it seems, by the Masonic ideals of humaneness, reasonableness, equality. His biographers have rightly objected to the widely accepted charge that he became, and remained, a Freemason because he was enmeshed in a time of troubles of his own, and that he valued his brothers for their wealth as well as their generosity – toward him. In fact, his Masonic loyalties and his need for money coincided; the second was not the cause of the first. Still, it is true that not long after Mozart joined the Freemasons, idealism and practicality conveniently merged.

5 THE BEGGAR

ON NOVEMBER 20, 1785, Mozart addressed a humble request to his brother Freemason, the publisher and composer Franz Anton Hoffmeister: "I take refuge with you, and beg you to help me with only a little money, since at the moment I need it very badly."[1] Yet, financially speaking, it had been a fairly good year for him; he must have earned some three thousand florins, at least twice as much as a respectable family needed to survive in Vienna. This frantic trawling for money would not be the last, and his requests grew more abject until his last year, 1791, when he enjoyed a partial economic recovery and his morale improved.

Admittedly, the Hapsburg establishment did little for him. In November 1787, Mozart was appointed *Kammermusicus* at the court of Joseph II. He had his foot in the imperial door at last, but the plum was small and sour; it helped less than he had hoped. His duties were minimal – to supply dances for an annual ball at the Redoutensaal – but so was his salary: eight hundred florins a year. "Too much for what I do," he is reported to have said bitterly, "too little for what I could do." He could not help knowing that Gluck, who had held this post until his recent death, had received the munificent salary of two thousand florins. This was another blow to his self-respect, to what he called his "credit."

No wonder that through the years, the Viennese have had to swallow the reproach that their callous indifference to the city's greatest genius allowed him to drop into shameful poverty and to be buried in an anonymous pauper's grave. There is something to this charge, but it is only a small part of the story. Mozart was not a prudent manager. It has been reasonably argued in his defense that it cost more to live in Vienna than in Salzburg, and that Mozart had to meet exceptional expenses, such as his wife's frequent stays at a spa to wait out one of her pregnancies or to cure unspecified ailments. But there were luxuries he refused to do without even when his cash, and his state of mind, were at their lowest ebb.

Nearly all the decade he spent in Vienna, then, Mozart should have been able to live on his earnings; they were more than enough to take care of himself, his wife, and his two surviving children. Writing to his father in January 1782, after he had been on his own for half a year, he worked it out that a married couple who wanted to live quietly, "as we wish to," could make do with about twelve hundred florins a year. It seemed to him in those confident first days that he could manage this minimum easily enough. If he just took one more pupil, he mused – he then had three – he would make something over one hundred florins a month.

He blithely counted on other resources: "I can write at least one opera a year, I can give an 'academy,'" a concert for his own benefit, "once a year, I can have things engraved, issue things by subscription."[2] He fully expected, too, that the concerts he would be giving at the palatial town houses of aristocrats would provide a substantial bonus. Yet his earnings soon proved insufficient to meet his needs as he understood them. Maynard Solomon's meticulous accounting of Mozart's income during the Vienna years leaves no doubt that in all of them, he earned a great deal more than the 1,200 florins he had postulated as necessary for a respectable existence: at least 3,700 florins in 1784 and 3,300 florins in 1787, probably more. Even in his least prosperous years – 1788 to 1790 – he never made any less than 1,400 florins.[3] But distraught, often humiliating appeals for funds became a habit with him.

For all the enthusiastic approval of highly connected amateurs in Vienna, the adoring tributes that Prague's music lovers paid their favorite composer, or the emperor's public gestures of applause, Mozart had no position better than *Kammermusicus* in sight. And so he continued to give lessons, an activity that, we know, he never liked. It could also be, as he portrayed it, a hazardous one – *as he portrayed it,* for at least one exceptionally graphic report to his father may have been a none too subtle fiction to demonstrate how scrupulous he was with women: one unattractive but persistent pupil who, he wrote, sweated like a peasant girl and let him see far more of her ample contours than he wanted to see, pursued him relentlessly: "You can plainly read: *I beg you, look here;* it's true, there is enough to see to make one want to go blind."[4] Yet he protested that he had no choice but to suffer unwelcome attentions of this sort; his father had not been altogether misguided when he had worried over Mozart's unsettled financial outlook. Even though his income in Vienna far outstripped the salary he had received at Salzburg, somehow it was never quite enough.

His son's lavish manner of life was all too obvious to Leopold Mozart; in February 1785, on a visit to the Mozarts, he reported to Nannerl: "You can surmise that your brother has handsome quarters *with every decor appropriate to a house* from the fact that he pays 480 fl. rent," more than triple the sum he had laid out for an earlier, more modest apartment.[5] Whatever Mozart craved, he bought; in this inability to resist his desires, and this inability alone, he remained something of a child. He spent considerable sums for a specially built piano; he prepared for tours with expensive handmade shoes and fashionable clothes; he had apparently convinced himself that daily intercourse with a social elite made a carriage a sheer necessity; he found that the pressure to relax made it imperative for him to keep a horse.[6] One of his essential luxuries was a billiard table; speaking as a witness, his biographer Niemetschek recalled that "he loved playing billiards passionately."[7] This extravagant style was the way to the nobility's esteem – to appear not as a hired hand or an insolent upstart, but as a cultivated artist, an equal to his hosts at least in the domain of music. In Mozart's mind vanity and status anxiety were intertwined.

As sober realities offered his vanity repeated checks, his anxiety only mounted. There were times during these last years when Mozart's monetary woes, or what he interpreted as such, turned him into a pitiable figure, all the harder for him to bear given his pride and self-awareness. He knew a begging letter when he saw one, but that did not stop him from writing them. In those days, Mozart suffered bouts of depression and could no longer conceal them from those who were close to him. Niemetschek recalled that in his last year, already sickly, Mozart fell into "somber melancholy."[8] It was not a new mood; the year before, writing to his wife, he spoke of his childlike joy at the prospect of seeing her again, and added, "If people could see into my heart, I would almost be ashamed – everything is cold to me – ice cold."[9] The longing for his wife's touch, maternal and arousing alike, coupled with his depression shows that his wants were more than merely pecuniary.

In despair, Mozart approached his brother Freemason, the well-to-do manufacturer, merchant, and private banker Michael Puchberg. Until Mozart's death, Puchberg remained his most dependable, though not his only, creditor – most dependable even though he usually sent less than Mozart had asked for. Mozart's pleas testify to a debilitating stress, a virtual collapse in his self-respect. "Dearest Brother!" he opened the first of his letters to Puchberg in June 1788, "Your true friendship and brother love embolden me to ask you for a great favor," a loan of one hundred florins, which Puchberg duly remitted.[10] Around the same time, he felt encouraged to open his heart and to propose a scheme by which Puchberg would lend him – "at an appropriate rate of interest" – one thousand or two thousand florins for one or two years, to give him a sense of safety. "Surely you yourself must find it *certain* and *true* that it is nasty, indeed impossible, to live when one has to wait from earnings to earnings."[11] As he had often told Leopold Mozart when he felt beleaguered by his father's inter-minable complaints and reproaches, he needed a certain serenity to do his composing. Unwilling or unable to respond to Mozart's stratagem to find emotional security through financial security, Puchberg sent two hundred florins.

The letters of the following year were, if anything, more groveling still. On July 12, 1789, he dispatched to his "dearest, best Friend" a forlorn message: "God! I am in a situation that I would not wish on my worst enemy; and if you, best friend and brother, desert me, I am lost, *unhappily and innocently*, together with my poor sick wife and child." He, too, had been ill and unable to work, but was getting back to composing and had bracing prospects in view. He asked for five hundred florins and added a scheme for repayment.

This was so self-abasing a solicitation that Mozart held on to it: "Oh God!" he added in a postscript two days later, "I can hardly make up my mind to send this letter! – and yet I must!" He closed with a broken phrase more eloquent than any of the coherent appeals he had made before: "Adjeu! – Forgive me for God's sake, only forgive me! – and – Adieu! ——."[12] When Puchberg did not reply instantly, Mozart returned to the attack on July 17: "Surely you are angry with me, because you are not answering me!"[13] Puchberg responded with 150 florins. Mozart salted his begging letters, though they were mainly tales of domestic illnesses, impatient creditors, and unproductive work with outlines of profitable commissions to come and with promises of prompt repayment. In the early spring of 1790 he reminded Puchberg, as though he needed reminding, that for some time "you will have noticed something sad about me all the time," and Puchberg sent 150 florins.[14] Through these years, Puchberg kept Mozart supplied with money – about 1,000 florins in all. But by the spring of 1791, the worst was over, and Mozart's requests for loans had decreased to modest sums, at times as little as 20 florins.

What had happened to Mozart's state of mind? Apart from a few touching outbursts about his travail, Mozart was not very introspective, at least not on paper. He had no doubt good reasons for sober reflections about his spending habits. His inability to hold on to money was incurable. In March 1785, visiting in Vienna, Leopold Mozart told Nannerl that his son had disposable funds and that his household, as far as food and drink were concerned, was run quite economically.[15] But what the Mozarts saved on groceries, they spent on shoes, servants, and billiard tables.

A shift in Mozart's musical interests also affected his income. In the mid-1780s Mozart turned his attention to that most demanding of genres, opera, and largely deserted his reliable source of income, the concerts at which he played his own concertos. We know that Mozart generally composed in spurts, writing concertos, quartets, sonatas, even operas, in clusters. And the financial rewards for his major efforts, though he could count on considerable added income from repeat performances, were limited: the original fee he received as composer of *Le nozze de Figaro* was 450 florins, and he earned the same with *Don Giovanni* and *Così fan tutte*. But a benefit evening of *Don Giovanni* in Prague gave him an added 600 florins. There was urgent need for the Mozart household, then, to review its budget, but from a rational perspective, no need for panic. The tone of Mozart's begging letters and his poignant testimony that he was feeling isolated and prey to constant sadness far outstrip the Mozarts' pecuniary realities. The principal source of Mozart's depression must lie elsewhere.

The most likely candidate as the cause of Mozart's misery is his lifelong contest with his father. During these years of sublime compositions and private anguish, their conflict grew more contentious than ever. Leopold Mozart's abrasiveness and self-absorption, far from diminishing as he advanced in years, only intensified. Not that the father failed to appreciate his son's music; as we have seen, he took great pride in it, to the point of tears. But his own needs remained paramount. No doubt, Mozart's spectacular triumphs in Vienna and his intimacy with the powerful, which his father was compelled to witness on that visit in early 1785, were so many insults to Leopold Mozart's pride. Mozart entertained, and was entertained by, Vienna's leading families; he knew everyone of note, including the emperor; he shook immortal compositions, it seemed, from his sleeve. Certainly when it came to music and sheer fame, the son had outdistanced his father with sovereign, almost contemptuous ease. He was leading a life of which his father could only have dreamt.

But in more intimate confrontations the aging Leopold Mozart exacted his revenge; he could still mobilize some effective sallies into the enemy's territory. We have noted it before: he never really forgave his son for spurning his advice – insistently, almost violently, offered – in escaping his father's direct domination by moving to Vienna. Again, marrying Constanze Weber in August 1782, once more defying his father's strenuous objections, did nothing to repair the widening breach between the two men. That his son should take a wife – even though he was twenty-six – was, to Leopold Mozart's mind, yet one more loosening of already fraying ties that had kept his son yoked to him in a kind of psychological immaturity.

In consequence Leopold Mozart progressively distanced himself from his son and instead cultivated an intimacy with his daughter, who had married in the summer of 1784. He even took over the care of Nannerl's first child, a son inevitably named Leopold, and faithfully began his letters to the infant's parents with a bulletin that became a refrain: "Leopoldl is healthy" or "Leopoldl thrives." Yet he "forgot" to tell his son that he was bringing up his grandson as his own. In tune with this secrecy mongering, he refused to accept Constanze Weber as a full member of his family despite her polite efforts, never showed the slightest interest in Mozart's children, or the slightest sympathy for the couple's distress at losing four of them in short order. It was almost inevitable that under these circumstances, brother and sister, who had been the most affectionate companions from their early childhood, should drift apart as Nannerl took her father's side.

An incident of November 1786 illuminates Leopold Mozart's partiality. Thinking of restoring his financial equilibrium, Mozart planned a tour of England and wanted to take Constanze along. Hence he asked his father to let his surviving two children live in his house for a while. Leopold Mozart took this request as an impudent demand, which he promptly rejected in the fiercest terms. But his combativeness had begun to lack zest; he was seriously ailing, and, aware of it, his son wrote him worried and philosophical letters. "Since death," he told his father in April 1787, "to be precise, is the true final purpose of our life, I have for several years made myself so well acquainted with this true, best friend of mankind that his image does not just hold nothing terrifying for me any more, but much that is soothing and consoling."[16] The following month, Leopold Mozart died at the age of sixty-seven, sincerely mourned by both his children.

At last, he left the son he had loved and tormented for so long. But he abandoned the scene of battle having implanted in his son irreparable feelings of guilt and an awareness of emotional and financial obligations left unfulfilled, obligations that would continue to plague Mozart as long as he lived.

Mozart's sheer weariness with life, then, the self-destructive elements in his sadness, appear like a battle continued, all the more desperate now that his antagonist was gone. There was now nobody at least to hear (if not listen to) his filial protests. Even through his last will, which favored Nannerl, Leopold Mozart made it plain that he remained unreconciled to his son. Here was material enough for dark thoughts. And here was material, too, for Mozart's disproportionate distress at his "poverty," a distress that made him write those undignified begging letters for loans. He wanted money from one creditor to satisfy other creditors. Was he not his father's son? He emphatically remained so even more vehemently after his father's death. Leopold Mozart had taught Mozart that to fail to repay loans promptly was to lose one's credit, and to lose one's credit was to lose one's honor. The father, even more powerful in death than he had been in life, had, it seems, won the duel after all.

And yet, except for some brief pauses, Mozart was composing more superlative music than ever. Worn down by his tribulations, haunted by "black thoughts," Mozart's resilience never quite abandoned him. He kept exploring with a sizable menu of dances, minuets, divertimentos, arias, and most of a requiem. He composed his last three piano concertos.[17] More astonishing still, these were the years he wrote his three greatest symphonies and his greatest operas.

6 THE MASTER

THE UNFOLDING of Mozart's genius is a history of steady, at times meteoric, growth. In his late adolescence, he composed some of his most enduring music, which he wisely refused to "improve" on in later years. One thinks of the A-Major Symphony, No. 29, of 1774 (K. 201); the last two of his five violin concertos, written in rapid succession when he was nineteen; and, above all, the Sinfonia Concertante for violin and viola of 1779 (K. 364). They have the incomparable Mozartian flavor, and point to his mature work.

But even after these masterly compositions, Mozart continued to soar. Felix Mendelssohn wrote the lovely overture to *A Midsummer Night's Dream* at the age of sixteen, and eighteen years later fitted it seamlessly into the incidental music for Shakespeare's fairy play. Franz Schubert composed "Erlkönig," the ballad that first secured him a measure of recognition in Vienna, when he was seventeen, and it is indistinguishable in sheer sophistication and mimetic inventiveness from the celebrated vocal compositions he wrote a dozen years later. Such inability to surmount an already high plateau was not Mozart's way. In short, as his father had already observed in Mozart's early youth, he never stood still; in the last six years of his life, from 1785 on, he poured out masterpiece after masterpiece that scaled greater heights and plumbed greater depths – how puerile these common metaphors are compared to the experience of *listening* to Mozart! – than any he had reached before.

There is an all-too-well-known melodramatic tale about Antonio Salieri poisoning Mozart. It began as a rumor and was first given literary form in the 1820s in a verse playlet by Pushkin. It is a malicious, preposterous fabrication, but hints at the envy Mozart's rivals had every right to feel. Yet Mozart, too, had grounds for envy: Salieri, born in Italy but long settled in Vienna, occupied privileged posts that Mozart would have deserved but, given Emperor Joseph's predilection for Salieri, could never hope to obtain. In 1774, Salieri was appointed court composer and conductor of the Italian opera, and did his duty in grand style: he wrote some forty operas during his tenure. Then in 1788, the year that Mozart wrote his three last symphonies, Salieri was further promoted to court kapellmeister. The Mozarts, father and son, accused Salieri of "cabals" to keep Mozart's operas from reaching the stage; but Salieri and Mozart were cordial enough acquaintances, if scarcely friends, and we know that Salieri conducted some of Mozart's compositions. And in October 1791, just before Mozart's fatal illness, he took Salieri to *Die Zauberflöte* and reported to his wife that his guest had overwhelmed him with extravagant compliments.

As usual, Father Mozart was far more vicious about Salieri than his son. In 1785, he heard Salieri's *La fiera di Venezia*, an opera buffa, and wrote to his daughter that it "hurt" him, "because it is in fact old-fashioned, artificial, and lacking all harmony," an *"arch-stupid"* piece of childishness.[1] It is true that Salieri was a conservative composer who around the turn of the century had to watch as his style lost popular appeal. His operas are all but forgotten. But during Mozart's lifetime, Salieri pleased, and not the emperor alone.

In the last five or six years of his life, then, amid the most untoward circumstances – competitors more in the court's graces than he, lack of steady employment, financial straits, uncertain health – Mozart worked almost without interruption at the top of his form. If his biographers have found it worth noting that in 1790 he wrote "merely" one string quintet, his last three string quartets, an adagio and allegro for mechanical organ, and *Così fan tutte*, this output seemed meager only in comparison with his natural pace. He wrote music that would make later generations hail him with ecstatic exclamations, and drive them to clichés purloined from the vocabulary of religion. If he had only lived just a few years longer! the lament goes. Would he have become a Beethoven before his time? – a much-canvassed conjecture, understandable but really pointless. He would have continued to be Mozart. The world of music lovers must rest content with what he gave it.

He gave it much in those last years, more than ever: it is the string quintets, the "Jupiter" Symphony, some late piano concertos, *Don Giovanni* that live most vividly in the collective musical memory. Never before in the history of Western music, and never since, has a composer crowded into so short a time so many masterpieces in so many genres. Not even Beethoven or Schubert would match Mozart in his sheer versatility.

One technical resource, apart from sheer freedom of

expressiveness, helped to shape Mozart's late compositions: his increasingly frequent and increasingly subtle use of counterpoint. "The art of counterpoint," as Walter Piston tersely defined it in an authoritative study, "is the art of combining melodic lines" that features the tension between two or more melodies and its resolution.[2] Luxuriating in the interplay of melodies in accord with exacting rules was anything but new. It had dominated the late-sixteenth-century polyphonic school of Palestrina and risen to the summit of transparent complexity (if one may put it that way) in the works of Johann Sebastian Bach. We recall that the adolescent Mozart had taken instruction in counterpoint from the great Martini in Bologna during his Italian tours and, partly on his father's urging, had written a few canons and fugues just to show that he had mastered the intricacies of strict rules. But then his attention had turned elsewhere.

We have seen how Mozart rediscovered Johann Sebastian Bach during his first year in Vienna. And his wife, enchanted with the Bach fugues he brought home, vehemently supported his new enthusiasm. When he confessed to her that he had been playing fugues on his clavier but had not written them down, she berated him for failing to immortalize "the most artistic and most beautiful of all music," and was appeased only when he sat down and wrote a fugue for her.[3] In the end Constanze Mozart was probably more enamored of strict counterpoint than her husband; how strongly his exposure to Father Bach resonated in his last compositions remains open to discussion. This much, though, seems plain: it augmented his compositional ammunition, powerful as it already was, and called for real mastery of the technical vocabulary. But Mozart was not just a follower of Bach:

whatever counterpoint he employed, notably in the great G-Minor Quintet and the equally great C-Major Symphony, he adapted to his style and made his own.

It was in the late piano concertos, his chamber music, symphonies, and operas that Mozart's final phase announced itself most conspicuously. To many admirers of his music the piano concertos represent him at his best. And it is true: whether in the last analysis listeners prefer his late symphonies or his operas to them, six or seven among his mature piano concertos can make a forceful claim to being the most Mozartian music of all. Interestingly enough, Mozart himself praised them for their appeal across boundaries of taste: they stand, he wrote his father in December 1782, "as intermediates between too difficult and too easy – are very brilliant – agreeable to the ear – naturally without dropping into vacuousness – here and there, *connoisseurs alone* can find satisfaction – but in a way – that non-connoisseurs can be content with them without knowing why."[4] He had good grounds to be proud of them: he had taken the genre from rudimentary beginnings to establish it, virtually singlehandedly, to still unsurpassed eminence. What Haydn had done for the string quartet, Mozart did for the piano concerto.

He wrote altogether twenty-seven of them, starting precociously with four concertos in 1767 at the age of eleven, when his composing was deeply indebted to Johann Christian Bach. As we have had occasion to observe, the young Mozart elbowed his way to originality by taking the path of intelligent appropriation. But youthful and derivative as these ventures are, they have certain flashes of their own. Like the concertos he would write in his late twenties and early thirties, they are in three movements – fast, slow, fast – but short, taking less than fifteen minutes. K. 175, written late in 1773, the ninth in the great sequence, was the first wholly of his own devising.

The gaps between Mozart's apprentice efforts, middle-period compositions, and late masterworks yawn wide, and he achieved the astonishing caliber of the last eight or nine of these concertos by leaps rather than gradual movement: as was customary with him, he bunched them into groups. Starting in 1784, largely living off his performances, he produced one sublime exemplar after another, four in less than three months, and fourteen in two years. The most splendid works, Nos. 18 to 25, are the product of that time, with two more in 1788 and early 1791 for good measure. Even though listeners probably have a favorite among them – most likely No. 20 (K. 466) or 24 (K. 491) – the concertos virtually all cluster at Mozart's highest level.

These late concertos are about twice as long as his first ventures. In their sheer grandeur of conception, their melodic and harmonic invention, they resemble his late symphonies more closely than they do his first piano concertos. Though they bear an unmistakable family resemblance, they have their marked individuality. Mozart's ability to generate a congenial, civilized musical conversation, which makes his mature chamber music such an enjoyment, found exceptional room for play in his piano concertos. The solo piano and the orchestra are partners, not rivals. That Mozart's endowment included a solid dose of a genius for drama is obvious enough in his operas, but it plays no less exhilarating a part in these concertos.

Visiting Vienna in early 1785, Leopold Mozart, though by now used, though never quite calloused, to his son's amazing gifts, was almost overcome by the two new piano concertos – Nos. 20 and 21 – that his son was performing to stormy applause. Especially the former, K. 466, roused him to the highest commendation in his vocabulary: he pronounced it "excellent – *vortrefflich*."[5] Even the German Romantics, who were not overly fond of Mozart's piano concertos, responded to what they liked to call its "demonic" power, with its key, D minor, and its growling, repeated, moody opening phrase. Demonic or not, significantly this concerto concludes not in a minor but a major key – Mozart was far too multifarious a composer to be easily captured.

It is only an apparent paradox that in the piano concertos of his final phase, this quintessentially sophisticated composer reached new pinnacles of simplicity as he stripped away grandiose gestures, which is to say acrobatic pianistic displays. Naturally these concertos have rapid runs and tricky leaps, but never for the sake of showing off the soloist's wizardry on the keyboard. Precisely what made nineteenth-century impresarios reluctant to put these concertos on the program – they gave the virtuoso too little spectacular work to do – was their supreme attribute. Among others, the middle movement of the Concerto No. 20 is an unimpeachable witness to Mozart's musical intentions: the soloist quietly announces the beautiful slow main theme, which the orchestra takes up; it could not be more artless – and more memorable. Other concertos, notably No. 24, share this uncluttered lack of embroidery. Played by the small orchestra he used – normally, as in No. 20, strings, two oboes, two bassoons, two horns, two trumpets, timpani – his music reached for utter transparency. In these compositions, Mozart elevated the arts of simplification and compression into new regions. Yet around the same time, he proved with his late operas that his register also included the most crowded sonorities.

In dedicating six string quartets to Haydn, Mozart observed, almost casually, that they were "the fruit of long and laborious toil." It is an arresting phrase. Mozart left ample testimony that he was capable of composing major works, to say nothing of minor ones, at uncanny speed. He wrote his last symphony, the celebrated "Jupiter," in sixteen days. The story that he composed the portentous overture to *Don Giovanni* the night before the premiere of the opera cannot be fully verified, but would certainly not have been beyond Mozart's powers. In other words, the stream of his musical inspiration seldom flowed less than swiftly or abundantly. And in emergencies he could mobilize his forces to exceptional efforts. During the fall of 1783, visiting old friends in Linz, he abruptly decided to give an "academy" on November 4. But, as he reported to his father on October 31, four days before the concert, he had brought no symphony with him. Hence he felt compelled to "write at headlong speed a new one, which has to be ready by then."[6] And it was.

At the same time, a meticulous examination of Mozart's autograph scores has disclosed that frequently the final drafts of his compositions were not the first ones; he would discard abortive openings or revise his texts with a critical eye.[7] Nor were his opera scores the only compositions to drive him to take a second look; they were only the most obvious candidates for revision, as he felt compelled to rework his score to fit unanticipated changes in the libretto or take into account the indisposition of an irreplaceable soprano. His last three string quartets, possibly intended for King Friedrich Wilhelm II of Prussia, a competent cellist, show considerable rewriting, second thoughts, perhaps fatigue. In short, Mozart performed the feats that his admirers called miracles mainly when the situation called for it.

In that age of well-trained and well-to-do dilettantes, composers wrote to gratify an importunate patron, an exigent soloist, an exceptionally gifted pupil; and in this practical professionalism Mozart did not differ from his rivals. "It is my wish and my hope," he told his father in May 1781, "to gain honor, fame, and money." Ten days later, he underscored that central fact of his life: "Apart from my health, I know of nothing more Necessary than money."[8] The widely accepted portrait of Mozart the lonely genius listening to his inner voices alone is a romantic distortion of the more mundane reality. Once he was moved to compose, inspiration took over, but the inspiration for that inspiration was likely a commission he had just received, a performance that required a new composition, a gift to an appreciative friend. Mozart lived among musicians, among performers, impresarios, and patrons, and tried to accommodate their tastes and their particular talents.

At times he composed as though to make reparation for his tasteless way with acquaintances. In 1783 he wrote the four concertos for horn and orchestra for the horn player Joseph Leutgeb, born like Mozart in Salzburg, a natural victim, whom it seems Mozart enjoyed tormenting with rude practical jokes but, at the same time, gave splendid opportunities to shine on his demanding instrument. For all his tough-minded pronouncements, he did not chiefly love music for the cash it brought him: "Privation teaches one to esteem money."[9]

It would be unwise to take these maxims at face value. They date from the spring of 1781, when Mozart was trying to persuade his incredulous father that moving to Vienna was a fiscal coup rather than a caprice. Still, Mozart had built much of this practicality into his character, and in the late 1780s, he would fully appreciate the gravity of his saying that privation does indeed make the pursuit of money a primary concern. And so, violin sonatas, piano sonatas for two or four hands, horn duos, piano quartets, and clarinet trios were so many responses to his financial exigencies.

Among these chamber compositions, his late string quintets with a second viola stand out as the most memorable. He had tried his hand at this combination early on, in 1773, but it was not until fourteen years after that, in the midst of his final, finest phase, that he returned to it, with two sublime exemplars, K. 515 in C Major and its complement, K. 516 in G Minor, written as a pair. These two quintets, as the Mozart specialist Stanley Sadie has put it in full agreement with other students of Mozart, "represent a peak in his chamber music," and that peak was very high.[10]

These quintets leave little doubt that Mozart had a special affinity for the genre. It seems to have given him intense gratification to work with the harmonic range open to five players in shifting, often surprising, exchanges. Instruments pair up, form alliances, echo one another, politely hand the main theme around and take it back, dissolve their partnerships to make way for new coalitions, all accomplished with a maximum of grace and a minimum of strain. In these quintets, Mozart took further steps to give the middle voices more work of their own to do; the violas and the cello too take the lead, with rich, deeply moving results. If Mozart's last two string quintets, K. 593 and K. 614, provide marginally less emotional satisfaction than the preceding pair, that is only because K. 515 and K. 516 were an act that even Mozart found hard to follow.

One reason Mozart's string quintets are among the most expressive among his compositions is the prominence of the violas. The viola was his favorite instrument. Though a virtuoso on the violin, in chamber groups he liked to take the viola part. And there is good reason to assume that he wrote the marvelous Sinfonia Concertante of 1779 with special engagement because one of the two solo instruments is a viola. In *La finta giardiniera*, that rather neglected opera of 1774, a central figure intones a love aria describing how musical instruments affect his moods. The flutes and oboes make him happy, the brasses and drums drive him to despair, the violas torment him with their somber melodies. There is, of course, no guarantee that a character invented by Mozart, and one not particularly attractive at that, speaks for its creator. But since this catalog is an incidental flourish, it seems trustworthy enough to reveal some of Mozart's responses to instrumental sounds. The "somber, tormenting" voice of the viola help to make these two quintets anything but happy music; there is something heartrending about them. In his authoritative study of the classical style, Charles Rosen has put it tersely: "The G minor Quintet is one of the great tragic works."[11] It is a wonderful instance revealing just how much beauty Mozart could wrest from melancholy.

The steep ascent of Mozart's development revealed in the progressive refinement of his chamber music is, perhaps, even more marked in his symphonies. In the course of his short life, he wrote more than fifty symphony-like compositions, some of them now lost. Traditionally the "Jupiter" Symphony, the last, is listed as No. 41, and this format sets Mozart's true symphonies apart from the *galant* divertimentos and serenades to which he turned for some years in the mid-1770s. By the time he wrote his last three symphonies, he had lost most of his interest in composing much as sheer diversion.

If anything, Mozart's output of 41 symphonies was moderate; Joseph Haydn, for one, is credited with 108 of them – though, of course, he lived to the age of seventy-seven. There was incessant demand for them; Vienna's concertgoing public counted on a symphony at just about every orchestral performance. Doubtless as a legacy from its early history as an overture, it was normally the first piece of music on the program, a placing that composers disliked and struggled to change. With good reasons: the opening number in a concert could expect to be disrupted by "listeners" noisily settling in and by thoughtless latecomers. But it *was* an indispensable ingredient in programming. "The symphony," wrote the German composer and critic Johann Abraham Peter Schulz around 1770, "is particularly well suited for the expression of the great, the solemn, and the sublime," whether it serves to introduce other compositions or stands by itself.[12]

We recall that Mozart wrote his first symphony in 1764 at

the age of eight and promptly followed it up with several more. Though they served him chiefly as exercises in a recently established if flourishing tradition, he endowed several of them with individual touches: for his Symphony No. 6 (K. 43), completed in the fall of 1767, Mozart added a minuet – a kind of declaration of independence from the symphony's parent, the overture. He would adhere to this four-movement pattern except for a few striking reversions – like the "Prague" Symphony – in his later symphonies. In the words of the eminent Mozart scholar Alfred Einstein: "We may characterize briefly the path of the symphony, as Mozart handled the form, from 1764 to 1788, as the path away from a work whose purpose was to furnish the frame for solo performances or concertos, to one forming the principal composition, the center and climax of a musical program. It is an advance from the decorative to the expressive, from the external to the internal, from mere ceremonial to spiritual avowal."[13]

As was his way, Mozart composed his symphonies in irregular clusters. As an adolescent, between 1769 and 1773, he wrote some thirty of them, as though he were trying to outdo his own record for fast composing. Ingredients in an overall pattern of intensifying inwardness and mounting musical effectiveness, these symphonies show progress over their immediate predecessors in their sheer mastery. Listeners have detected in them Mozart's felicitous absorption of Haydn's recent symphonies: one master learning from another. But then, preoccupied with other forms and facing diminished opportunities to have his symphonies performed in Vienna, Mozart the symphonist slowed down. Still, in 1782, he wrote the charming, *galant* Symphony No.

35 (K. 385), the "Haffner," as appealing as any he ever did; the "Linz," already mentioned; and, in 1786, the superb "Prague" Symphony for his beloved adoring musical public in that city. And he closed his vocation as a symphonist in 1788 with three breathtaking works.

Mozart composed these symphonies (K. 543, K. 550, K. 551) in a headlong rush, taking only about two months for all three of them together. The impulsion for these masterworks remains obscure; no commission, no plans for an "academy" in Vienna, have come to light. But it seems unlikely that Mozart, an eminently practical craftsman, would expend all this energy without at least pondering a future performance; it seems possible that he intended them for concerts in Vienna during the winter season or, more adventurously, in London – a tour he contemplated but never took.

Whatever their reason for being, their reputation over the decades has only soared; they are indisputably his most magnificent symphonies, indeed among the most magnificent symphonies in the literature. Mozart did not conceive them as a trio; none echoes the other two. All they have in common is his genius at its summit. Hence the listener can keep them apart. "One of the most significant differences between Mozart's last three symphonies," the English music critic Donald Francis Tovey has observed, "concerns the characters of their themes. In the E flat Symphony [No. 39] the themes are evenly poised between formulas on the one hand and attractive melodies on the other, with euphony always paramount. In the G minor Symphony [No. 40] almost every theme is highly individual and, even when formal in phrasing, quite unexpected in its course. In the last symphony [No. 41, the "Jupiter"] we reach what is really the final subtlety of an immensely experienced artist."[14] This final subtlety includes Mozart's choice of making the last movement, traditionally a kind of cheerful wrapping-up of a symphonic composition, into a long, stunning climax.

Students of Mozart still debate the place of the "Jupiter" Symphony in the history of music in general and in Mozart's oeuvre in particular. Some have been unable to resist the temptation of regarding it as a grand parting statement, Mozart's farewell to the world and his farewell to a post-rococo classicism that was to be followed, and overthrown, by Beethoven's Promethean, heaven-defying symphonies. But that is to yield to overinterpretation. It is better to regard the "Jupiter" Symphony simply as a particularly ripe fruit of Mozart's late style. He was sending no messages, conveying no sense of finality. Had he lived longer, he would probably have written more symphonies, and we have no way of fathoming what they would have been like. Georg Nikolaus von Nissen, who, we remember, married Mozart's widow and published an important biography of Constanze Mozart's first husband, called it "truly the first of all symphonies. In no work of this kind does the divine spark of genius shine more brightly and beautifully. All is heavenly harmony, whose tones, like a great noble deed, speak to the heart and enrapture it; all is the most sublime art, before whose power the spirit bows and is amazed."[15] This is praise ladled onto the canvas of commentary with heavy impasto and not quite to our more acerbic taste. But it was perhaps the best that educated nineteenth-century listeners, struggling to convey their emotions on hearing the "Jupiter," could come up with.

After all, even seasoned twentieth-century musicologists, professionally averse to being caught in sentimentality, have found these symphonies, especially the "Jupiter," so far beyond criticism that ordinary language has often failed them. "The third symphony of the trilogy, K. 551, has been aptly nicknamed *Jupiter*," writes Philip G. Downs in a substantial survey of classical music.[16] There has been speculation that it was Johann Peter Salomon, the impresario who lured Haydn to London, who invented the name; its first printed use occurred in 1822.[17] "For as Jupiter was the father of the gods whose weapon was the lightning bolt and thunder," Downs continues, "so the symphony wields superhuman power and moves with sovereign ease through the biggest symphonic architecture of the century. The first movement contains a wealth of material, completely disparate and ranging from the majestic to the trivial; from the terrifying to the tender. Its effects range from the humorous to the intellectual in the creation of an exacting first movement, and yet it is in the fourth movement, justly famous as one of the greatest technical *tours de force* in all of music, that the listener is overwhelmed. Here, several short motives are fashioned into a web of counterpoint, without parallel in its vigor and strength. It is Jupiter-like, or Jovian, in that its dazzle and power can hardly be comprehended, any more than its technique can be apprehended; it can only be wondered at."[18]

Played in chronological order, then, Mozart's symphonies display his characteristic evolutionary pattern. With the passage of years they grew longer, unfolding from a mere slip of a composition taking all of ten or twelve minutes to the robust adult masterpiece lasting a solid half hour; they became more imaginative, coupling a bubbling melodic fertility with the most audacious possible way of playing with his inventions. The dissonances and chromatic shifts Mozart so brilliantly deployed provided his astonished listeners with moments of simple poignancy or sheer delight; as a whole they manifest a concentrated power that puts Mozart's earlier orchestral work into the shade. He wrote these symphonies around the time he completed *Don Giovanni,* and the same largeness of musical thought informs them both. To experience them is to enjoy a spectacle of energy translated into beauty. The repetitions, the cross-references, the themes and their modulations are joys of rare purity; the last movement of the "Jupiter" Symphony concludes with a complicated fugue that combines five subjects into a stunning climax. All this provides eloquent evidence for the particular amalgam of playfulness and seriousness that was Mozart's hallmark.

Still, from the beginning, and for decades after, Mozart's last three symphonies had a mixed reception. Much of the public found them "difficult." Leopold Mozart would have agreed. Enchanted as he was with his son's music, he, too, had thought it hard to enjoy easily, certainly at first hearing. Joseph II, a well-informed dilettante, thought so, too, as did vocal segments of concertgoers. For them Mozart was a "learned" composer, and they did not intend this epithet as a compliment. Even those who professed particularly to admire the G-Minor Symphony disagreed about why they did so. Robert Schumann, almost as well known in his day for his music criticism as for his compositions, spoke for a nineteenth-century majority when he called this work the incarnation of classical harmony, "Hellenic hovering grace." But, although a case can be made for this reading of the G-Minor Symphony, it is far from being a complete interpretation. Serenity was one ingredient in the mix, but so was passion, and so was musical technique applied with complete confidence and no sign of strain.

It is vulgar to read music as a simple translation of its composer's moods or a literal response to private events. A slow movement in a minor key by no means indicates that the composer was unhappy when he wrote it, any more than a jaunty air guarantees a merry frame of mind. Without independent biographical information, one cannot legitimately draw a direct connection between life and work. Mozart's music, especially in its final phase, was beautifully expressive, relatively free of formulas. He was no Tchaikovsky, who virtually invited his listeners to recognize, if not quite share, his deep depressions. We know this much: Mozart was not permanently despondent; even in his debt-ridden years, when he complained of sadness and feelings of emptiness, he could live for the moment with real gusto; he could play cards, indulge in a round of billiards, dress for a great occasion, work out a practical joke. The portrait of an invariably morbid Mozart is as much a caricature as that of a childishly exuberant one.[19] But, ever more obtrusively in those years, the ground tone of his life became that of the viola.

7 THE DRAMATIST

AS HIS LIFE'S WORK richly attests, Mozart felt at home with virtually any type of music his contemporaries were producing, from elevated to scatological – masses to canons on the invitation to kiss his ass. "As you know," he told his father in 1778, "I can pretty well assimilate and imitate all sorts and styles of compositions."[1] No doubt he could, but by that time he was almost done assimilating and imitating and was writing what everyone could recognize as "pure Mozart." Only Johann Sebastian Bach still awaited his discovery, some three or four years later. His catholic range, though, did not keep him from cherishing a special passion, early and late, for sung dramatic dialogue – preferably set to music by himself. In 1764 his father reported from London that his son "constantly has an opera running in his head, which he wants to perform in Salzburg with all sorts of young people."[2] Mozart was then eight years old.

Seven years later, in November 1771, when father and son were in Milan, Mozart demonstrated his prodigious memory for his favorite genre: he recalled an entire opera by the respected composer Johann Adolf Hasse, a feat obviously far more taxing than remembering shorter, less teeming compositions. He told his sister that on the evening he was writing her, one of Hasse's operas was being performed, but his father was not going to attend, and he could not go out by himself. "Fortunately I already know just about all the arias by heart, and so I can hear and see it at home in my thoughts."[3] Such casual reports helped to establish the legend that Mozart always had complete compositions in his mind before he had set down a note.

His craving for operas, particularly for composing them, obsessed Mozart all his life. In 1777, he confessed to his father, "I only have to hear people discuss an opera, I only have to be in a theater, hear tuning up – Oh!, I am quite beside myself right away!"[4] Early the next year, he sounded, if anything, more avid, more imploring still: "Don't forget my wish to write operas," he reminded Leopold Mozart. "I envy everybody who is writing one. I could actually weep with vexation when I hear or see an aria."[5] By the mid-1770s, he already had half a dozen operas, or operatic experiments, to his credit. His first, we know, had been *La finta semplice*, an opera buffa written when he was twelve; since then, with *Mitridate* and *Lucio Silla*, he had conquered the domain of opera seria, grandiose and elevated. His major operas, starting with *Idomeneo* in 1781, were still to come.

In the unending debate over the respective importance of music and libretto, Mozart was an unequivocal, highly partisan champion of music. He summed up his thoughts epigrammatically: "In an opera," he told his father in October 1781, while he was at work on *Die Entführung aus dem Serail*, "the poetry must positively be the obedient daughter of the music." After his youthful impetuosity to set almost any text had abated, he knew what he needed: "It is best when a good composer who understands the stage and is himself able to suggest something, gets together with a clever poet as a true phoenix."[6] He might have been describing himself and his most accomplished librettist, Lorenzo da Ponte, with whom he would write *Le nozze de Figaro, Don Giovanni*, and *Così fan tutte*.

Mozart granted that a librettist with a felicitous pen could make a real contribution to an opera's stature; but an opera with creditable music and an absurd, erratic libretto was still worth saving – Mozart's own *Zauberflöte* was a case in point – while an opera with inferior music but a fine libretto belonged on the rubbish heap. Finding a good librettist, though, was no easy matter; the field was overrun by mediocrities. "I have easily looked through 100 – yes, probably even more librettos," Mozart complained to his father in May 1783, "but I have found scarcely a single one with which I could be satisfied."[7]

Mozart did not hesitate to judge such matters confidently; he thought of himself as a "composer who understands the stage." He was a true man of the theater, and a perceptive one. A substantial cache of evidence confirms his self-appraisal: a series of letters dating from late 1780 to early 1781, written while he was completing *Idomeneo*. While Mozart was working with the singers in Munich, his hand-picked librettist, Giambattista Varesco, a chaplain in Colloredo's court, was in Salzburg. So was his father. And eager to profit from Leopold Mozart's professional counsel, Mozart would write to him and have him transmit his recommendations to Varesco. These suggestions, meticulous and detailed, document Mozart's secure feel for drama, his impulse to drive the action forward, interrupting it only when absolutely necessary. On occasion, he would add an aria to gratify a self-promoting or friendly soprano or tenor, but even then he tried to integrate these favors into the action. And everything, he insisted, in speech as in music, must be as natural as possible.

To that end, working on *Idomeneo*, Mozart refused to countenance spoken asides, which of course were appropriate to a Singspiel rather than an opera seria; vetoed one aria because it made the movement of events appear "limp and cold" and would compel the other singers to stand around awkwardly on stage; wanted another aria reduced to a recitative. He tried to remedy any possible confusion that a noisy ensemble might cause in the audience; his motto was lucidity above all. Although a few times he asked Varesco to add a few words to the libretto, nearly always he thought that speeding up the plot was a substantial gain.

Mozart could be ruthless in serving the cause of dramatic effectiveness. In the last act of *Idomeneo*, an oracular voice issues portentous commands and leads the opera to its happy ending. Varesco's version of this crucial intervention struck him as loquacious: "Tell me," he asked his father, "don't you think that the speech of the subterranean voice is too long? Consider it well. – Imagine the theater; the voice must be terrifying – it must penetrate – one must believe that it is really there. – How can the speech manage that if it is too long? Its very length will more and more persuade the audience of its nullity." And he gives the apparition of the elder Hamlet, the murdered king of Denmark, as an instance: "If in *Hamlet* the speech of the ghost were not so long, it would be even more compelling. – This speech here, too, is very easily shortened, it gains more from that than it loses."[8] Varesco's efforts to accommodate the masterful composer were evidently unsatisfactory, and Mozart simply took action on his own. "The oracle's speech is still much too long – I have cut it," he confided to his father. "Varesco doesn't need to know anything about this, for it will be printed just as he wrote it."[9]

No composer has ever been more thoroughly schooled than Mozart, and his technical competence was equal to any task. Beginning at home with his exigent father-teacher, continuing with the lessons of Padre Martini, absorbing the influences of Johann Christian Bach, Joseph Haydn, and, from 1782 on, Johann Sebastian Bach all spurred on his genius. But it was the dramatic needs of opera that brought all his talents, all his training into play. As we have seen, other compositions, notably the late piano concertos and the late symphonies, had given his dramatic gifts ample room for expression. His operas made the fruits of those gifts all the more visible.

One felicitous ingredient in Mozart's well-schooled, controlled passion for the theater was his ability to write *characteristic* music for voice. In doing so, he realized the contemporary aesthetic ideal of opera, after all in essence a drama with music as its central expressive means. Though thoughtful of the particular strengths and limitations of each performer with whom he worked, he was even more concerned to have them sing the kind of music one might expect from the attributes they were embodying on stage and from their driving internal energies: commanding, almost snarling for Count Almaviva in *Figaro*; simple, mock-innocent for Zerlina in *Don Giovanni*; florid, expansive for Fiordiligi in *Così fan tutte.* One wonders what kind of plays Mozart might have written if he had not been so busy composing operas. They would certainly have been highly dramatic.

In May 1783, Mozart told his father about a "certain abate da Ponte" who had just been appointed poet to the Italian Theater in Vienna, and who had promised to "make something new" for him. In his official capacity, Mozart acknowledged, da Ponte had an enormous amount of work on his desk, and his first duty was to write a libretto for Salieri. But once that was done? Mozart was skeptical: "Those Italian gentlemen are civil to your face! – enough, we know them!" And if da Ponte should reach a good understanding with Salieri, he added, he – Mozart – would not get a libretto out of him as long as he lived. He sincerely regretted this: "I would really like to show myself also in an Italian opera."[10]

For once, Mozart's pessimism proved unjustified: two months later da Ponte presented him with a text and Mozart thought he might take it if "he will carve it up in accord with my views."[11] Nothing much came of this enterprise; Mozart briefly tinkered with an opera, *Lo sposo deluso*, and then set it aside. But a year later, when Mozart and da Ponte began to adapt Beaumarchais's play *Le Mariage de Figaro*, which had been a sensation in France, their historic collaboration was born.

Da Ponte was a fascinating partner. His life adds up to one long escapade, filled with scandals, hasty moves from country to country, and the most varied accomplishments. It seems only fitting that one of his friends should have been the adventurer, author, and peripatetic lover Giacomo Casanova. He was born in 1749 in the ghetto of Ceneda near

Venice as Emmanuele Conegliano; fourteen years later, his widowed father had his three sons as well as himself baptized to permit him to marry a young Christian woman. Largely self-taught in his early youth, Lorenzo da Ponte, as he was now known (having taken the name of the bishop who had baptized him), elected to prepare for the priesthood. This was the most promising way of making up for lost years in his education and, at the same time, securing a step up the social ladder. But it soon became plain that the newly minted da Ponte had no vocation for the austere life of a priest, although he did take minor orders. He wanted to be a poet and a man-about-town; after moving to Venice in 1773 and leading a licentious life, he became both. His adulterous affairs got him into trouble with the law, and he fled northward; in 1782, he settled in Vienna in search of patrons who would assist his career. He was fortunate, or gifted and adroit, enough to make a good impression on Salieri and on Emperor Joseph II himself. His appointment as official poet to the Italian Theater followed soon after.

Then came the glorious Mozart years, but by 1791, the year of Mozart's death, da Ponte thought it prudent to be on the road again. He vagabonded through Western European capitals, proposing and trying out intriguing schemes for theatrical ventures, which, all of them failures, mainly resulted in the need for more schemes. To earn his keep, he worked as a translator, wrote librettos for lesser composers, and published his poetry. For several years he hovered precariously in London, where he worked as the poet for the King's Theatre in the Haymarket as a librettist, and foundered in debt. By 1805, he surfaced in the United States, with a wife and five children in tow, throwing himself into his accustomed commercial and financial games. His last years were most rewarding: in 1825, at the age of seventy-six, he was appointed professor of Italian at Columbia University. He died in 1838, four decades after Mozart, leaving behind an interesting but unreliable autobiography in which he gives himself more credit for Mozart's three imperishable comic operas than he probably deserved.

The precise respective shares in the making of these operas must remain obscure unless some documents unexpectedly turn up. That da Ponte was a poet with an accurate ear for dialogue and an impressive feel for drama is certain; but Mozart, the man of the theater, did more than write the music. Whatever the truth of the matter, by 1785, the two were at work on *Le nozze de Figaro*, which they described as a "commedia per musica."

It was a bold and clever choice. Beaumarchais had battled for almost a decade with the French authorities for permission to stage *La Folle Journée, ou Le Mariage de Figaro*. He had completed the comedy in 1778, and it had found favor with highly placed personages. It had even been privately performed. But it was not published and publicly acted until 1784, for to the nervous censors whose task it was to clear all publications, it seemed far too disrespectful in its portrayal of Count Almaviva, an overbearing, philandering – and jealous – aristocrat and, in contrast, overly appreciative of Figaro, the Count's valet, and Suzanne, personal maid to the Countess. Figaro and Suzanne are engaged to be married and want to persuade their master to forgo the long outdated feudal privilege of enjoying the bride on her first night of marriage – the *jus primae noctis*. The Count had voluntarily surrendered that right but, appreciating Suzanne's charms, wanted to revive it. The play turns on his desire and its frustration. Once it reached the Comédie-Française, it proved a triumph. Its part in provoking the French Revolution has been greatly overstated – at St. Helena, Napoleon said that the comedy was already the revolution in action – but it was a diagnosis of a society riven with irreparable social tensions.

In their version, da Ponte and Mozart followed Beaumarchais's comedy with fair fidelity, using most of the characters' names, only translating them into Italian. Like the play, the opera has Figaro and Susanna intriguing to have the bride enter matrimony with her honor – that is, her virginity – intact; their master, with ideas of his own on this subject; his charming, long-suffering wife; the nubile Cherubino, in love with all the women within his reach (played, according to Beaumarchais's instructions, by "a young and very pretty woman," an idea da Ponte adopted for the opera); Marcellina and Bartolo, plotting to blackmail Figaro into marrying Marcellina but turning out to be his parents instead; and assorted spear carriers.

The story of Figaro, too, and the essential social attitude that had made the play such a hit largely reappeared in the opera: the Count's indefatigable attempts at seducing Susanna, the young woman's keen intelligence and frankness, the convolutions involving false identities and an amiable conspiracy to teach the Count a lesson. And drama and opera alike were markedly egalitarian: The Countess and Susanna are not perfect equals – neither Beaumarchais nor Mozart was an extremist – but they are affectionate friends as well as mistress and servant; no composer has ever written a duet for female voices sweeter than the one Mozart composed for the confidential talk between the two as they concoct a letter that will trap and shame the Count.

Da Ponte, who had persuaded Joseph II to let him work on *Figaro*, proceeded despite its rebellious subtext, only toning down Beaumarchais's erotic allusions and suggesting, rather than spelling out, the Count's regrets for having abandoned his privilege to enjoy the bride's body. The libretto's most striking departure from its model was a cut in a fervent speech Beaumarchais had written for Figaro in the last act. In a rage, Figaro, wrongly convinced that his beloved Suzanne is betraying him with the Count, breaks out against the fickleness of women and then turns to berate his master: "No, Monsieur Count, you will not have her . . . you will not have her. Because you are a grand seigneur, you think you're a great genius! Nobility, fortune, rank, appointments, all that makes you so proud! What have you done to deserve so many advantages? You took pains to be born, and nothing more. For the rest, quite an ordinary man!" And he sharply contrasts his own learning and accomplishments with the Count's meager record.[12]

It is a great speech, the longest in Beaumarchais's play. But da Ponte thought it expedient to drop this political diatribe and to concentrate instead on Figaro's misogynistic advice to all men to be on guard against women: Open your eyes! Watch out for their treacherous nature! Da Ponte left a good deal of realistic class conflict in his libretto for *Figaro*, and sharp erotic tension as well; in his famous first-act aria "Se vuol ballare," Figaro virtually challenges the Count to a duel over Susanna. But for the most part da Ponte softened these strains, especially the sexual ones, beneath the glittering surface, although Mozart saw to it that they audibly pervaded the action with all their raw élan. In arias, duets, trios, sextets, and the stylish commentary emanating from the orchestra, at moments sinister, more often sarcastic, always supremely melodic, Mozart conjured up real human beings on the stage, plagued by passions, hobbled by inconsistencies, struggling with power and themselves.

In the end, understanding conquers misunderstandings; Susanna and Figaro will proceed with their wedding; even the Count is brought to apologize for his sensuality and his gratuitous jealousy. How long his remorse will last is uncertain, but the opera ends before it can be tested. The worry about the future is irrelevant; *Le nozze de Figaro* contains some of the most searching and most enchanting music Mozart ever wrote. In 1881, Johannes Brahms, a close student of his predecessors' music, remarked to a friend, "Every number in Mozart's *Figaro* is a miracle to me; I find it absolutely incomprehensible how someone can create something so absolutely perfect; nothing like it has ever been done again, not even by Beethoven."[13]

The Viennese, though, were not persuaded of the opera's perfections. They heartily applauded at the premiere and asked to have several numbers repeated; but after a few performances, *Figaro* disappeared from Vienna's repertory, not to return until 1789. *Una cosa rara* by Vicente Martín y Soler, with a libretto by da Ponte, first performed a few months after *Figaro*, easily outdrew Mozart's great comedy with its simple, whistleable music and stereotyped characters. It is now almost forgotten.

Prague was different. In December 1786, Mozart visited the city to attend performances of *Le nozze de Figaro*. He had good friends in Prague, and these were happy days, a welcome relief from the gloomy thoughts that had been troubling him for some time. In January 1787, he reported to a friend how pleasant it was to see people cheerfully dancing to music from *Figaro*, which they had converted into contradances. "Here, people talk of nothing but – *Figaro*; nothing is played, blown, sung, and whistled but – *Figaro*; no opera visited but *Figaro* and all the time *Figaro*. Certainly a great honor for me."[14] Mozart was scarcely exaggerating. Prague's musical public, wrote Niemetschek, himself from Prague, was well equipped to appreciate Mozart's genius. "My *Prager* understand me," Mozart is reported to have remarked, with justice. Without any audible dissent, the Prague public was taken with Mozart, with *Figaro*, with his piano improvisations on tunes from *Figaro*, with his "Prague" Symphony, a prologue to the level that the last three symphonies, still to come, would conquer. The visit was a welcome boost to Mozart's finances: he netted no less than one thousand florins. Just as gratifying, Pasquale Bondini, Prague's most enterprising impresario, offered Mozart a contract to write an opera for the winter season.

That opera was *Don Giovanni*. Premiered in Prague in late October 1787, it received, Mozart wrote a friend, "the loudest applause."[15] It was a *dramma giocoso*, a genre virtually invented by the prolific Italian playwright and librettist Carlo Goldoni that mixes elevated with popular elements. In fact, there is precious little pure mirth in *Don Giovanni*; whatever humor we find – apart from the conventional portrayal of Leporello, vulgar and shrewd, the comic servant of theatrical stereotypes – is laced with a certain viciousness or unapologetic hedonism. Some of the opera's best-known set pieces could only scandalize conservative moralizers. One thinks of Leporello's famous "catalog aria," in which he lists for the benefit of the horrified Donna Elvira, one among many of the Don's discarded mistresses, the types and the number of women the Don has enjoyed in his travels – hundreds in country after country, "but in Spain, already a thousand and three." One thinks, too, of Don Giovanni's short, explosive so-called "champagne aria" (in which champagne is not mentioned), which extols nothing better than pure – which is to say, impure – pleasure. Beethoven, who is on record as admiring Mozart's music for *Don Giovanni*, shuddered at the thought that he could ever write an opera on a subject so lewd. The last day on earth of an unregenerate, licentious aristocrat struck him as unworthy of semicomical treatment.[16] Yet the censorious have never carried the day.

As they had done with *Le nozze de Figaro*, librettist and composer turned to literature for the plot, this one with a long and lively pedigree; the story of the irresistible, impious libertine punished in the end went back two centuries in various versions. It was a major challenge for the Mozart–da Ponte team as it explored momentous issues – attempted (or actual) rape, murder, blasphemy, and damnation. At the heart of *Don Giovanni* lie the insatiability and the vagaries of sexual urges, as they had in *Figaro*; but *Don Giovanni*, far more candidly than *Figaro*, exhibits their links to aggression and, as well, the pathetic loyalty of a lover, Donna Elvira, throwing herself away on an unworthy philanderer. Yet with all its seriousness, *Don Giovanni* is neither static nor stately; as a *dramma giocoso,* it displays a certain raucousness, as it pursues the protagonist's course from crime to punishment through swiftly progressing and interlocking sets of incidents. The Don makes continuous new attempts at seduction; plays bewildering games of mystification; has unsettling encounters with Donna Elvira; exhibits an extreme disregard of conventional morals; and bravely defies the supernatural avenger.

Da Ponte's models, the plays and librettos written about the Don Juan legend, were too brief to yield a full-fledged opera without some padding, and he eked out the plot with some ingenious, scattered set scenes: this was one time that Mozart sacrificed speed for length. Musicologists have received these interpolations with some reserve: strictly speaking, several episodes, especially in the second, last act, do not materially advance the story. But the music Mozart wrote for them ranks among the high points of this opera, and more than makes up for some untidiness in the Don's rush to his doom.

The ominous, emphatic opening bars of the overture telegraph to the listener that grave business is about to unfold. "From the beginning of the Overture," Charles Gounod wrote in his adoring commentary on the opera, "Mozart is completely in the spirit of the drama, of which it is an epitome. The first chords, so powerful and solemn with their syncopated rhythm, establish at once the majestic and formidable authority of Divine justice, the avenger of crime."[17] The opera starts without pause after the overture; the first character on stage is Leporello, Don Giovanni's servant, delivering himself of an angry outburst against his master as he stands guard outside a mansion belonging to the Commendatore. Then, after this complaint, which tells us as much about the Don as about Leporello himself, the opera plunges into the midst of the action. Don Giovanni and Donna Anna, and then her father, the Commendatore, emerge from the house; in the darkness of night, the Don has tried to conquer, or actually has conquered, Donna Anna.

Scholars disagree on this less-than-vital issue. Those who favor the more drastic prehistory point to Donna Anna's extreme fury. (Had she been saving herself for, or perhaps expecting, her fiancé, Don Ottavio? Had she secretly enjoyed what morals and religion must condemn?) Whatever happened before the curtain rises, the Don duels with Donna Anna's father and mortally wounds him. After the Don and his servant effect their escape, the frantic daughter hastily reappears with Don Ottavio, whom she has summoned, and tells him just what has happened. With hysterical intensity, more than once, she makes him swear to avenge her.

As though nothing has happened, Don Giovanni tries to seduce the pretty, unsophisticated peasant girl Zerlina, who is at a feast celebrating her impending marriage to Masetto. Half inclined, half tempted by the Don's smooth persuasions (no composer ever excelled Mozart in setting ambivalence to music), she ponders his promise to marry her, starts to go off with him, but is saved by Donna Elvira and will eventually secure Masetto's forgiveness. In the closing scene of the first act, Donna Anna and Don Ottavio, seconded by Donna Elvira, confront the Don, convinced that he has murdered the Commendatore, but he escapes once again.

The second act has the Don and Leporello walking through a cemetery and coming upon a massive statue of the Commendatore; it seems to have been designed and constructed within an hour or two – but, then, this is opera. Impudently, the Don, ignoring Leporello's pleas to be more respectful, forces him to invite the monument to dinner. With a nod and a deep "Sì," the Commendatore accepts, setting the stage for what many seasoned music lovers have come to prize as the most powerful scene in all opera.

The climax takes place, appropriately enough, in Don Giovanni's elegant chambers, where he is presiding over a giddy dinner. The scene is not without humor as Leporello wolfs down some of the food intended for the Don's guests, and these light moments make the tragedy about to happen all the more gripping. In the background an orchestra plays excerpts from contemporary operas, including Martin's *Una cosa rara* and Mozart's own *Figaro*, on which Leporello drily comments that he knows that tune all too well. Raising his glass, the Don hails women, wine, and freedom. Donna Elvira rushes in, beseeching him for the last time to change his life and save his soul, but he shrugs her off. Then, as she leaves, she utters a shriek: she has seen the statue approaching.

The Commendatore enters, superhuman in size and paralyzing in authority, and a duel for the Don's soul ensues. For all the statue's urging, Don Giovanni remains impenitent; even after it takes his hand, making him shiver to the bone, he persists. "Repent, change your life," the statue orders him. "Change – this is your last chance!" But the Don faces his executioner, insolent to the end: "No! Old fool!" The exchange grows ever more laconic: "Repent!" "No!" "Repent!" "No!" In a last effort to persuade the sinner – in which Leporello joins from his place of safety under the table – the statue demands: "Yes!" But the Don, rising to heroic stature, utters his final rejection with a tone that only a high baritone can reach: "No!" He may be an unscrupulous and blasphemous libertine, but he stands by the way he has spent his days and nights: Long live women, song, and freedom! And the statue takes the Don down to hell. One need hardly add that Mozart's orchestration, using solemn trombones for the first time, matches the rising, almost unbearable suspense to perfection.

Mozart's *Prager* who were at the premiere in October 1787 were not disappointed in "their" *Don Giovanni*; but Vienna was, as so often with Mozart, more critical. In mid-May 1788, after making some revisions, Mozart staged the opera there and enjoyed only a modest success. Opinions were divided; some thought the music "agreeable and very varied," but more complained that it was "learned" – an epithet, we know, that was not a compliment – and the opera-loving emperor, who had returned from the front as the Hapsburgs' Turkish war dragged on, commented that Mozart's "music is certainly too difficult for the singers."[18]

From the outset, *Don Giovanni* was bedeviled by debate, not least about the closing sextet that follows immediately upon the Don's final fall. Donna Anna, Don Ottavio, Donna Elvira, Masetto, Zerlina, and Leporello gather on stage and give a relatively bland account of present sentiments and future plans. Given the wonderful shock of what has just happened, this scene has struck many listeners as an anticlimax. No doubt it considerably lowers the emotional temperature. To leave the opera house just after the statue has contended for the Don's salvation and lost would produce – or, rather, sustain – a Romantic mood. And Romantics (like Gustav Mahler after them) frequently dropped the sextet. The uncertain tradition that when Mozart staged *Don Giovanni* in Vienna, he too left it out, gave this cut a certain prestige. But it is unjustified, however appealing it may be on dramatic grounds. Mozart was not writing a Romantic opera, but a *dramma giocoso*, which traditionally required, much like a novel by Dickens, a finale to tie up loose ends:

Zerlina and Masetto will resume their wedding feast, Donna Elvira will retreat to her nunnery, Donna Anna begs an impatient Don Ottavio to wait a year before they marry, and Leporello will of course look for a new master. It is appropriate that the opera should close in a major key.

If *Don Giovanni* left the pure in heart feeling uneasily that Mozart and da Ponte were celebrating immorality (or at least moral ambiguity) by making a compulsive philanderer into an existential hero, the last opera on which the two collaborated, *Così fan tutte*, had after its opening triumph an even more adverse reception. It came to be widely condemned as breaching the bounds of decency.

The comedy originated in a command performance: Joseph II had been preoccupied with the Turkish war, but after listening to a revival of *Le nozze de Figaro* in Vienna, he requested that Mozart write another opera buffa. He even suggested the subject, rumored to be the retelling of a recent incident in Vienna. This meant that da Ponte, though he could consult a few literary ancestors, had to work largely with his own imagination. He acquitted himself splendidly; Mozart seems to have felt inspired, rather than, as some have said, weighed down by da Ponte's plot. The cast of characters the two came up with was perfectly – perhaps too perfectly – balanced: two young, eligible officers, Ferrando and Guglielmo; two young, beautiful sisters, Fiordiligi and Dorabella, engaged to these officers; an elderly cynic, Don Alfonso, abetted by Despina, a smart, worldly ladies' maid.

The action starts with a rush as the two men, very much in love, praise their fiancées' fidelity to Don Alfonso, who refuses to believe a word of it: women are too flighty to be faithful. They make a bet and will prove (or disprove) the women's steadfastness by staging an elaborate hoax: Ferrando and Guglielmo pretend to be called to duty, and in a touching scene they say farewell to the sisters. With Don Alfonso assisting, the four lovers sing a poignant quintet that rises above the immediate, rather farcical occasion to illuminate the pain all lovers must feel when they part.

Ferrando and Guglielmo soon reappear, improbably disguised as Albanians in comic-opera uniforms and impressive mustachios; with Don Alfonso acting as their sponsor, they beg to be introduced to the ladies, who at first refuse, being too miserable to see company. Persuaded by Despina and piqued by their own curiosity, they admit the Albanians, and soon find them intriguing – each pairing up with her sister's fiancé. Pretending to be dying of love, the Albanians drop to the floor. A doctor is summoned – it is Despina, equipped with a gigantic magnet, an amusing satire on the current fashion of Mesmerism. Chattering in some mystifying jargon and making passes with her magnet, the "doctor" promptly draws out the fluid that is about to kill the Albanians.

In the second act the sisters succumb, after virtuous expressions of fidelity and, then, stabs at delay for decorum's sake in arias that try to explain their inconstant feelings. Left alone with Don Alfonso, who has won his bet, the disillusioned officers raise their voices to shout out their misogyny: *Così fan tutte!* – Thus do they all! – *Così fan tutte!*

A marriage contract is drawn up and a notary (Despina again, this time as a nasal and breathless tenor) appears to solemnize the bond. Then, abruptly, Don Alfonso announces to the sisters that their former fiancés have unexpectedly returned. Their utter fickleness is exposed; but all ends well, the men forgiving and the women forgiven. A last puzzle remains, one that, given the lack of instructions from Mozart or da Ponte, is in practice insoluble and hence resolved according to the director's inclinations: do the original couples resume where they had left off before the men had departed, or do they persist in the new pairing? Does it matter? In this puzzling minuet of love – if one may call it love – one solution is as good, or as trivial, as the other.

The Viennese audiences who attended the premiere and the repeat performances early in 1790 found nothing to disapprove of; what mattered to them was what they saw as the wit of the words and the beauty of the music. But detractors, acknowledging the beauty while discounting the wit, controlled opera productions throughout most of the nineteenth century. They did not hesitate to tinker with the score and insert other Mozartian arias; but for the most part, eager to preserve as much of the music of *Così* as they could safely manage, they substituted what they considered to be less offensive language or concocted wholly new librettos. In 1863, French operagoers were offered a version titled *Peines d'amour perdues* that took as its model Shakespeare's *Love's Labour's Lost*, which shows some resemblance to *Così*. Then, gradually, conscientious musicians restored *Così* to its original state; in Munich in 1897, the great Wagnerian conductor Hermann Levi saw his own translation of da Ponte's text performed (in Germany, until relatively recently, all operas were sung in German) in a new production that was all Mozart.

Yet no Mozart opera continues to divide professional listeners as widely as does *Così fan tutte*. For Edward Dent, an authority on Mozart's operas, the book is "the best of all da

Ponte librettos" and indeed "the most exquisite work of art among Mozart's operas." In sharp contrast, Joseph Kerman notes in his highly regarded *Opera as Drama* that "there is something unsatisfactory about *Così fan tutte.* Certainly it is Mozart's most problematic opera," and he refuses to be mollified by interpretations that try to rescue it, whether seeing it as a witty exhibition of the geometry of love, a lighthearted fairy tale, or an exposé of the shallowness of courtship in a declining Old Regime.[19]

Così fan tutte, defying the moralists, made its way across Europe – like Mozart's other major operas – though not into the United States, where it did not make its first appearance until 1921. In retrospect, it looks like a belated valentine to the Old Regime. While in early 1790, when *Così* was first performed, the French state was beginning to buckle under the pressure of evolving events – political infighting, the disastrously declining reputation of the royal house, looming bankruptcy, ominous popular participation in politics – the French Revolution, just half a year under way, did not yet appear as the epochal break with the past it would soon be seen to be. There was still time for audiences to be frivolous, especially when frivolity was being served up by a genius.

Yet acceptance of *Così fan tutte* in Vienna did not depend on operagoers' indifference to politics. There was the playful and seemingly inexhaustible loveliness of the music; it was, as students of Mozart have long noted, awash in ensembles. Edward Dent, who has counted them, notes "eleven arias, six duets, five trios, one quartet, two quintets, one sextet, and two huge finales, each of which includes every possible combination of voices."[20] The listener can readily imagine Mozart taking pleasure in his virtuosity, and understand the lovers of his music who have not hesitated to call *Così fan tutte* a perfect opera. While the controversy over *Così fan tutte* goes on, there are those who think, reasonably enough, that this opera is one of the most delicious pieces of music he ever wrote.

Mozart's last two operas, first performed in the closing year of his life, could not have been more different from the three he had written with da Ponte: they return to the operas he had composed a decade before. *Die Zauberflöte* is a Singspiel, sung in German and with spoken intervals, much like *Die Entführung aus dem Serail*, though far more profound; *La clemenza di Tito* is an opera seria that surpasses its predecessor, *Idomeneo*. It is as though Mozart were completing a circle, revisiting his initial triumphs on the stage. Naturally, these concluding compositions were on a different level of accomplishment; the Mozart of 1791 was no longer the Mozart of 1781. But the family resemblance is as striking as the advances he had made.

In *Die Zauberflöte*, the listener must struggle to understand – or, perhaps better, to set aside – the plot for the sake of the music. Mozart's librettist was Emanuel Schikaneder, manager of a theater specializing in staging popular amusements done in German. He had risen from utter poverty by his own abilities; violinist, actor, librettist in turn, he had shrewdly learned to appreciate and exploit the Viennese penchant for fairy tales set to music and for colorful productions set in unidentified, and often unidentifiable, exotic places. Bits of the supernatural and broad humor were much sought after in these folksy operettas. Some time early in 1790 Schikaneder developed an idea that appealed to

Mozart, even though he recognized that by composing an opera for an impresario catering to the multitude, he would be joining company socially far inferior to his usual circles. But he needed the money, since the new emperor, Leopold II, who had succeeded Joseph II upon his death in February 1790, seemed disinclined to offer Mozart any profitable commissions.

Once engaged in the project, Mozart intended *Die Zauberflöte* to rise above the stuff Schikaneder usually presented to please his boisterous audiences. Schikaneder was perfectly willing to go along. Like Mozart, he was a Freemason, and their opera would celebrate Masonic values and reenact a Masonic initiation into the realm of virtue, where Nature, Reason, and Wisdom hold sway. Hence the text is awash with solemn pronouncements about the essential equality of commoners and noblemen – both, whatever their rank, share the dignity of being human – with an ideology of noble restraint and the need to prove oneself worthy of joining the fraternity of rational humanists. Mozart's music has recognizable allusions to Masonic cantatas, including some of his own. Still, all this earnestness did not compel Schikaneder to forgo theatrical coups like savage, aggressive snakes, attempts at rape, paraphernalia with occult powers (like a magic flute that can soothe savage beasts and make them dance), mystical ceremonies, and grandiose staging that accommodated priests marching in solemn procession.

After drastic and confusing changes in the libretto, Schikaneder placed the action in ancient Egypt and made Sarastro, a deep bass, the spokesman for Masonic ideals; as a high priest of Isis and Osiris, he governs a fraternity much like a Masonic lodge. The hero, Prince Tamino, encounters the brotherhood as he searches for Princess Pamina, held captive by Sarastro, and with whom Tamino has fallen in love at first sight – of her miniature. "The portrait," he sings, "is enchantingly beautiful." Just as Don Giovanni needed Leporello by his side, Tamino finds a loyal, amusing, and boastful attendant in the birdcatcher Papageno, looking for a wife of his own.

The story is hopelessly convoluted and self-contradictory. It is enough to know that Tamino will be admitted to the Masonic fraternity, find his princess, and in her company, with her taking the lead, undergo a series of trials to test their mettle, including a period of silence. Unfortunately, Pamina (who has fallen in love with Tamino as promptly as he had with her) takes this as rejection and prepares to commit suicide – from which she is, of course, rescued. As expected, the loving couple triumphantly surmount the obstacles thrown in their way by the pseudo-Masons and are united forever. Papageno, too, will be granted his wish: Papagena.

The music carries it all, even though the incongruous conduct of Mozart's cast of characters and the flat humanitarian preachments made great demands on his ability to shift from one style of vocal writing to another: songs of love and longing that might have come out of Mozart's da Ponte period; comic songs that permitted a good deal of buffoonery on the stage; two notoriously demanding coloratura arias; and secular hymns. It was to these hymns that so irreligious a listener as Bernard Shaw responded: "I am highly susceptible to the force of all religious music, no matter to what Church it belongs; but the music of my own Church – for which I may be allowed, like other people, to have a partiality, is to be found in *Die Zauberflöte* and the Ninth Symphony."[21] Thus, whether listeners can tolerate the libretto or not, *Die Zauberflöte* has held its own in modern opera houses in the fierce competition for limited places in the repertory.

The opposite has been true of Mozart's swan song as an opera composer, *La clemenza di Tito*, which had a mixed reception at its premiere and is rarely revived today, although some of its set pieces still serve at recitals. Written in haste for the coronation of Leopold II as king of Bohemia in Prague, most of it in some three weeks, it boasts several fine individual numbers, the unusual employment of instruments like the basset horn, and an enlarged, strikingly dramatic role for the chorus. But none of this was enough to rescue the opera as a whole. It has been suggested that officials picked the libretto as a propaganda piece designed to counter the republican talk coming out of France by idealizing a legitimate ruler: the French Revolution was starting to capture the attention of the wider public in the Hapsburg lands. But quite apart from its possible political uses, the Freemason Mozart could not have wanted to quarrel with a drama in which benevolence is the central theme. The opera portrays the emperor Titus as chivalrous beyond the call of duty, almost of common sense; he pardons close friends condemned to death for mounting a conspiracy against him. Everyone sings ecstatic relief and the curtain falls. *La clemenza di Tito* celebrates grandeur, which includes the ability to forgive, the grandeur of legitimate power.

. . .

Though Mozart's operas cover a wide spectrum of subjects and of styles, they bear a marked family resemblance. The first shared quality was, it hardly needs saying, the splendor of his music, supported by the keen feeling for the drama that is alive in all his oeuvre. Even in less-often-performed efforts, there are jewels waiting to be excavated: a quartet in the third act of *Idomeneo*; or, in *La clemenza di Tito*, the conclusion of the first act, in which four principals and the chorus explore the inner turmoil of the conspirators.

Among Mozart's creations, his women rank among the most prepossessing. Throughout his career, Mozart wrote glorious music for sopranos, not simply to show off the singing prowess of the divas with whom he worked in Munich, in Vienna, in Prague, but also to embody interesting, often admirable characters. Reminiscent of heroines in Shakespeare's comedies, a Beatrice or a Rosalind, they match their men in wit, energy, and courage, at times outdo them. There was gossip, plausible but undocumented, about Mozart's supposed affairs with singers, notably with the English soprano Anna (called Nancy) Storace, who created the role of Susanna. True or not, in his operas Mozart showed himself an admirer of women. Blonde, Konstanze's maid in *Die Entführung aus dem Serail*, is an animated exemplar of the freeborn Englishwoman afraid of no one. Ilia, the heroine of *Idomeneo*, more than measures up to her lover in longing and fidelity alike. Donna Elvira in *Don Giovanni* may seem an unlikely candidate for this catalog; a hysteric with an undying love for Don Giovanni, she makes a slightly ridiculous figure. But, like the Don himself, she is a true individual; her anguish and her stubborn refusal to recognize her former lover's character are subtly observed; they speak of a woman clinging to the one experience in her life that has taken her out of her passive piety. It is Princess

Pamina in *Die Zauberflöte*, ready to kill herself if Tamino should stop loving her, who guides the prince through their ordeals. And Despina, the maid in *Così fan tutte*, belongs on this list. More truthful and forthcoming than her mistresses, whom she shocks by putting their illicit wishes into words, she is the one resourceful woman in the opera.

The most remarkable of them all is, of course, Susanna in *Le nozze de Figaro*. Though far less experienced in the ways of the world than her treasured Figaro, she is more perceptive than he about the Count's roving eye; with the adroitness of the society lady she is not, she keeps herself for her fiancé by consummately playing the game of flirtation with the Count; a little wicked in a good cause, in company with her friend the Countess, she organizes a little deception that will show up Count Almaviva and, on her own account, she arranges to punish Figaro, mildly, for his unwarranted jealousy. She is "only" a maidservant, if to a countess, but she carries herself with a dignity worthy of a bourgeois lady at her best. One wonders from what experiences or with what imaginative freedom (not forgetting da Ponte's help) Mozart invented so utterly lovable a young heroine – they are echoes, perhaps, of the young Constanze Weber or her sister Aloysia, whom Mozart loved before he noticed Constanze, or perhaps of some of the more intriguing sopranos he met on the road.

But an even deeper obsession seems to be driving Mozart's creative powers: the father-son conflict. Granted, this was a fairly conventional dramatic theme; granted, too, Mozart did not always discover, or originate, his plots. But his verve and the quick, sure touch with his operas makes it likely that the spectacle of combat between a father (or father figure) and a son (whether biological or psychological) pressed him to respond to its implications. The traits of the fathers in the libretti he set to music varied greatly: often a father is idealized, but others are defied, defeated, or self-destructive.

Evidently, fathers were much on the mind of Mozart the composer of operas. In *Idomeneo*, the king hands his royal power to his son, Idamante. In *Le nozze de Figaro*, Count Almaviva is exposed to deserved ridicule and is powerless to prevent, or to sully, the marriage of Susanna and Figaro. In *Die Entführung aus dem Serail*, Pasha Selim shows the loftiest generosity by allowing the young lovers in his power to marry even though he fancies the bride for himself. The subject was very much on Mozart's mind: the opera had its premiere in July 1782, and he married Constanze Weber a month later, against his father's un-Selim-like objections. And the emperor in *La clemenza di Tito*, we recall, is the soul of magnanimity – a paternal presence refusing to exercise authority that must have figured in Mozart's wishful fantasies. Only in *Don Giovanni* does the father take his revenge: parricide, whether wished for or real, must be punished. Leopold Mozart pursued his son even from the grave.

8 THE CLASSIC

THE END OF MOZART'S LIFE, like its beginning, spawned some hardy legends. This much we know: some time during the summer of 1791, perhaps in early August, a messenger brought Mozart a singular request. The letter was unsigned and the courier immovably discreet; every effort to discover the sender's identity, he warned, would prove futile. The unknown patron commissioned a requiem mass from Mozart, and Mozart, though very busy once again after the drought of the late 1780s, agreed to undertake the assignment.

Decades later Mozart's widow recalled his telling her that he was writing the Requiem "with the greatest pleasure, since it was his favorite kind of music; his friends and enemies would study it after his death" as his "masterpiece and swan song."[1] If this recollection is at all accurate, Mozart was being rather lavish with the word "favorite": we have good reason to believe that writing operas engaged his passionate attention more fully than anything else. But he certainly did not shrink from church music; considering his conditions of employment in the Salzburg years, he could hardly neglect it altogether. The Köchel catalog of his works lists some twenty complete or fragmentary masses, short and long, and more than a score of other pieces of church music. Granted, Charles Rosen has rather severely characterized most of Mozart's church music as "perfunctory, less profound and even less carefully written than the great secular works."[2] But the Requiem, a masterpiece of contrapuntal writing, was his most ambitious venture in the genre and by far the most powerful.

It retained its power even though Mozart did not live to complete his commission. He managed to set down much of the lengthy work, or to provide enough full sketches to enable another composer to add orchestration or voice parts with some ease. Still, he left gaps, especially in the latter half of the work: the Lacrimosa breaks off after a few bars, and Mozart seems not to have touched the three last movements – the Sanctus, the Benedictus, and the Agnus Dei – at all. Fortunately, his gifted pupil Xaver Süssmayr, a minor composer in his own right, filled in the gaps, attempting to make his contributions a mimicry of Mozart's late style. It is a tribute to his labors that his precise share in the Requiem remains a matter of some discussion. He had every right to think he knew what he was doing: several years after completing it, he recalled that he and Mozart had discussed the Requiem frequently, including the instrumentation, so that he had a good idea of Mozart's precise intentions.[3] Süssmayr aimed to be anonymous, indeed invisible, and to a large extent he succeeded.

Since this remarkable commission reached Mozart so close to his death – he died around four months after receiving that mysterious letter, on December 5, 1791 – most of his biographers have found the symbolism of the Requiem almost irresistible: a dying man writing a mass for the dead! Niemetschek, to whom we owe the first account of this affair, was also the first to engage in myth making. "On the day of his death," he writes, Mozart "had the score brought to his bed. 'Didn't I predict that I was writing this requiem for myself?' he said, and once again attentively perused the whole with moist eyes. It was a last painful farewell look at his beloved art – a premonition of his immortality!"[4]

This is "poetic" writing based on uncertain anecdotes; Niemetschek was not at Mozart's deathbed. That Mozart's music was destined for immortality seemed a safe prediction; contemporaries felt his death to be a serious loss and published encomiums of the sort he could have used during his lifetime. Joseph Haydn, better qualified than anyone else to appreciate the immensity of that loss, was in London at the time and wrote upon hearing the news: "For some time I was quite beside myself about his death. I could not believe that Providence should have called a priceless man into the other world."[5] Aspiring biographers started to gather material for a life of Mozart. Newspapers fished for choice adjectives to laud the greatest of masters and most celebrated of composers. Publishers launched projects for his collected works. And in Prague, always his city, the orchestra of the Prague National Theater advertised a solemn mass "as a mark of its boundless veneration and esteem," and performed it before large and appreciative audiences.[6]

Yet the story of Mozart's Requiem is more prosaic than Niemetschek made it. Apparently a few insiders knew the identity of the patron soon after Mozart's death – at least that is how they liked to remember it later – but it took some time before the "Anonym," as Mozart's widow consistently called him, was unmasked before a wider public. He was Count Walsegg, a fellow Freemason and acquaintance of Mozart's, who was amassing an oeuvre by quietly ordering works from several composers and then having them copied and played as his own at his regular private concerts. The commission for Mozart was by far the most extensive work Walsegg had ever "composed"; his wife had died early that year, and he wanted to present a requiem mass in her memory. Mozart was only the most distinguished of Walsegg's hacks. In short, there was nothing supernatural about the commission, nothing ghostly or portentous, only the sordid trickery of a rich and boastful amateur.

The last year of Mozart's life has often been described as one long preparation for death. But in that time, Mozart wrote two operas, a piano concerto, a large number of minuets and counterdances, a clarinet concerto, a Masonic cantata, two quintets, and most of the Requiem. His creativity was still working at full speed. In June 1791, he told his wife that he had written an aria "from sheer boredom."[7] He traveled; he conducted; he went to the opera several times a week. He still made scatological jokes; he delighted in news from Prague that *Tito* had been performed with "extraordinary applause"; he attended performances of *Die Zauberflöte* in Vienna, vividly enjoyed having numbers repeated and, best of all, "the *silent applause.*" We know that he took Salieri to *Die Zauberflöte* in mid-October and noted with pleasure that his guest had called it "worthy of being performed for the greatest festivities in front of the greatest monarch."[8] He continued to relish his food, his pipe, his billiards. He wrote his last letter to Constanze on October 14; he made the last entry in his register of compositions, a *Kleine Freimaurer-Kantate*, on November 15 – all signs of tolerable health. To judge from his letters, he was not a dying man until his last month.

In the light of Mozart's normal productivity, there is little difference in this pace from nearly all earlier years, except perhaps a more hectic speed. And this may be a clue to his state of mind; there is some suggestive evidence that he had come to use composing as an anodyne, as a remedy for melancholy and the pangs of loneliness in the midst of crowds. In a poignant letter to his wife of July 1791 – she was once again at Baden, her favorite spa, right outside Vienna – he gave vent to his solitude and an aching sense of an inner void: "You can't imagine how long all the time has been without you! I can't explain to you how I feel, it is a certain emptiness – which pains me – a certain longing which is never satisfied, consequently never ceases – persists and persists, indeed increases from day to day."[9] We have seen it before: he craved his wife's love not only in bed but as a maternal forgiving touch. But though he was often miserable, he was not dying.

Late in August 1791, Mozart, accompanied by Constanze and Süssmayr, traveled to Prague for the coronation ceremonies of Emperor Leopold II and to attend the premiere of *La clemenza di Tito*. And there, Niemetschek records, during his two-week stay filled with performances of his work, Mozart was sickly and in need of medication. "His color was pale and his expression sad."[10] Yet until October, amidst melancholy brooding, he seems to have been capable of his old playfulness, though by mid-month he apparently showed symptoms of mental distress, and his wife was not the only one to notice it. He seemed depressed and excessively preoccupied, plagued by obsessive ideas. He told his wife that he thought he had been poisoned, and she came to believe that the Requiem, on which he was working almost frenetically, had begun to assume the contours of doom for him.

This at least is how his widow said she remembered her husband's last weeks as she guarded, and sold, her increasingly famous husband's legacy – his manuscripts. It remains impossible to assess to what extent she was disclosing hitherto private information or contributing to the Mozart legend. Soon after she was widowed, she proved herself acquisitive and entrepreneurial, especially in her negotiations with Mozart's publishers. In her new situation as the relict of a recognized genius, she was not above dramatizing her late husband's life. In a word, she helped stimulate the rapidly growing Mozart industry and drew considerable financial advantage from it.

Mozart's terminal illness, however complicated by psychological malaise, was a physical disease: an attack of acute rheumatic fever. There has been as much controversy about Mozart's death as there has been about many aspects of his life, but scholars have arrived at a consensus that Mozart had suffered several episodes of rheumatic fever in earlier years, and that his last disease was a recurrence, in a more intense, possibly lethal form. On November 20, 1791, he went to bed with painful swellings in his arms and legs, found it hard to move his limbs, and suffered fits of vomiting. Fifteen days later his life was over.

So rapid a slide from health to death was no rarity in Mozart's age, but his very prominence stimulated fantasies among conspiracy theorists. Only a week after his death, a musical periodical in Berlin reported that some people at least believed that he had been poisoned. The slanderous story that an envious Salieri had poisoned Mozart arose only decades later, quite as preposterous as the original rumor. Indeed, if anyone murdered Mozart, it was his physicians, reputable and well-meaning eminences in Vienna's medical establishment: not yet impressed by the emerging opposition to bleeding, they reduced his body's resistance by repeatedly drawing blood and probably gave him blood poisoning with their unsterilized instruments.[11]

Mozart's doctors did their best by their lights; when Emperor Leopold II died some three months after Mozart, his physicians, too, bled him several times – bled him, a few enlightened critics asserted, to death. But the medical profession of the age acted from sadly misguided presuppositions about bodily functions and dysfunctions. And so when Mozart's physicians and their colleagues prescribed their deadly remedies, they more often exacerbated an illness than alleviated it. Mozart was only one of their most distinguished victims.

The mythmaking did not stop even after Mozart's death. As recent biographers have rightly insisted, the widespread belief that he was interred in some anonymous pauper's grave is without substance, and the picture of the unattended hearse being borne to the cemetery in a stormy winter night the stuff of melodrama. One can see why this caricature has enjoyed so long a life. There is something satisfying about the sorry spectacle of the genius neglected, something romantic about the contrast between the lonely artist and the philistine world in which he is forced to live, and die: Vienna's greatest artist buried without fanfare, without an iota of recognition – a supreme instance of a city's ingratitude toward one of its immortal sons.

The truth is rather different. Mozart died at a time when lavish and conspicuous funerals were severely discouraged, had in fact been the subject of a decree issued by Joseph II. The new simplicity, which did not exclude burial in common graves, was in tune with the anticlerical convictions and the contempt for "superstitious" ceremonials fostered by the thinkers of the Enlightenment and largely endorsed by rulers like the Hapsburg emperors. Leopold II – the brother of Joseph II, who had died in 1790 – in whose reign Mozart was buried, kept a number of his brother's edicts intact, at least for a while. What is more, though the cheapest of affairs, the interment was a degree – if only a degree – above pauper's grade. And from what we know of Mozart's convictions, steeped as he was in the Catholic Enlightenment with its touch of anticlericalism, and refined by his Freemasonic principles, we may deduce that he would have wished for nothing else.[12] There was less pathos in his end, sad as it was, than many have liked to think.

The sailing of Mozart's music through the waters of posterity was far from smooth. As we have noted, the contemporaries who mourned him were more or less clearly aware – Haydn more than anyone else – that a great composer had died. But with the passage of years, admirers of his music became rather selective with their praise. We have noted, too, that his piano concertos were not flamboyant enough to receive their due in an age of virtuosos and that there was a view widespread among operagoers that *Così fan tutte* was too frivolous, really too obscene, to be staged without major "improvements"; it took literally a hundred years before the opera would be performed once again in its integrity. In his *Mémoires*, Hector Berlioz, still smarting at the recollection, reported that French "morons" had desecrated Mozart's Overture to *Die Zauberflöte* by adding some bars of their own, and that they had "assassinated" Mozart with a tasteless rewriting of Don Giovanni's "champagne aria," converting it into a trio for bass and two sopranos.[13]

In this atmosphere, Mozart became the composer of *Eine kleine Nachtmusik*, that delectable, accomplished late serenade, but at least in comparison with his greatest compositions, relatively lightweight. Mozart came to be treated as a distant genius, a survival from the Old Regime, wigged and powdered, alien to a more Romantic, less "classical" age. In 1832, in a long letter from Paris to his teacher Karl Friedrich Zelter, Felix Mendelssohn raged against the local fashion of worshiping Beethoven by abusing his great predecessors: "I simply cannot stand the denigration of Haydn and Mozart, it drives me mad."[14]

Like Mendelssohn, other composers recognized Mozart's stature all along. Beethoven long thought Mozart's work beyond that of all rivals, though in his final years he came to place Handel first. Schubert stood in awe of "the magic sounds of Mozart's music."[15] Robert Schumann singled out Mozart as one of music's three geniuses, with Johann Sebastian Bach and Beethoven the other two. Chopin's predilection for Mozart was impassioned and enduring. So was that of Tchaikovsky, who credited Mozart with launching him on his vocation as composer. Brahms, we know, put the perfections of *Le nozze de Figaro* above anything that Beethoven ever accomplished. For Richard Strauss, Mozart was simply the "divine Mozart," and he refused to write about him: "I can only worship him."

It is interesting to speculate just how Mozart would have responded to these accolades, some of them downright blasphemous. As these pages have shown, he did not lack self-confidence. He knew himself to be a person of "superior talent" who would "do honor to any court." But a transcendent genius, perhaps the greatest composer who ever lived? Most likely he would have disdained the vulgar game of comparative rankings and been content to be in the company of Bach and Haydn. Yet he might have frowned at the patronizing criticisms launched against him in the age of Meyerbeer, Liszt, and Wagner for his classical distance and his supposedly lifelong childlikeness. His late symphonies and major operas continued to be performed, and he always had his enthusiasts, but the bulk of nineteenth-century music lovers treated Mozart as a charming precursor, a promise that Beethoven had amply fulfilled.

These reservations did not go unchallenged. By the 1890s the reaction against the reaction was well under way. Increasingly clamorous listeners, wearied by what they lamented as the bombast and pseudo-religiosity of Wagner and the Wagnerites, coined the heartfelt slogan "Back to Mozart!" Around 1910, Felix Weingartner, celebrated conductor and less celebrated composer, put the matter even more pointedly. Mozart, he wrote, was the answer to the malaise of recent music, but he would first have to be redis-covered before his role in the renewal of music could be fully appreciated: "Forward to Mozart!"[16] Somehow, it seemed, one had to grow into a full recognition of Mozart. In his autobiography, the great conductor Bruno Walter, particularly known for his sponsorship of Mahler's music, confessed that when he was a young conductor, Mozart, "who was later so thoroughly to dominate me and fill me with blissful happiness, was still somewhat alien to me. I was still unable to sense the seriousness in his charm, the loftiness in his beauty."[17] Post-rococo elegance was only the surface of Mozart's achievement. This perspective became the rule of the Forward-to-Mozart school: the more serious Mozart's music was recognized to be, the more seriously he was taken.

This turnabout has had its regrettable aspects. The feverish commercial activity intent on selling Mozart during his anniversary years has made him, like other objects of consumption, a plaything of the marketplace. It is sobering to think that Leopold Mozart would probably have strongly endorsed this hucksterism. But the comprehensive exposure of Mozart has also yielded dividends. It remains one of the achievements of which the dismal twentieth century can rightfully boast: it has raised Mozart's music – all of it – to the eminence it deserves.

NOTES

Chapter One

1. Johann Peter Eckermann, Gespräche mit Goethe in den letzten Jahren seines Lebens, in Goethe, Gedenkausgabe der Werke, Briefe, und Gespräche, 27 vols. (1949–64), vol. 24, 390, 373–74.
2. Ibid., 673.
3. Maynard Solomon, Mozart: A Life (1995), 53.
4. Ibid., 312.
5. Otto Erich Deutsch, Mozart: A Documentary Biography, tr. Eric Blom, Peter Branscombe, and Jeremy Noble (1965), 153–54.
6. Georg Niklaus Nissen, in Florian Langegger, Mozart, Vater und Sohn: Eine psychologische Untersuchung (1978; 2nd ed. 1986), 10.
7. Michael Kelly, Reminiscences (1826), quoted in Deutsch, Documentary Biography, 535.
8. Leopold Mozart to Lorenz Hagenauer, November 10, 1766. Mozart: Briefe und Aufzeichnungen, eds. Wilhelm A. Bauers, Otto Erich Deutsch, and Joseph Heinz Eibl, 7 vols. (1962–75), vol. 1, 232. Henceforth cited as Briefe. All translations are mine.
9. Leopold Mozart to his wife, February 3, 1770, ibid., 312.
10. Leopold Mozart to Lorenz Hagenauer, November 27, 1764, ibid., vol. 2, 176.
11. Leopold Mozart to his son, April 6, 1778, ibid., 334–35.
12. Leopold Mozart to Lorenz Hagenauer, October 16, 1762, ibid., vol. 1, 52–53.
13. Leopold Mozart to Lorenz Hagenauer, August 20, 1763, ibid., 90.

14. Franz Niemetschek, Leben des K. K. Kapellmeisters Wolfgang Gottlieb Mozart nach Originalquellen beschrieben (1798; 2nd ed. 1808), ed. Ernst Rychnovsky (1905), 13.

15. See Leopold Mozart's entries into his daughter's notebooks, Briefe, vol. 1, 48.

16. Leopold Mozart to Lorenz Hagenauer, October 19 and November 10, 1762, ibid., 53, 61–62.

17. Leopold Mozart to Lorenz Hagenauer, September 26, 1763, ibid., 94.

18. Leopold Mozart to Lorenz Hagenauer, February 1 and May 28, 1764, ibid., 123, 147–51, quotation at 149.

19. Leopold Mozart to his wife, May 26 and June 9, 1770, ibid., 352, 359, 360; to Lorenz Hagenauer, May 28, 1764, ibid., 147.

20. Leopold Mozart to Lorenz Hagenauer, September 26, 1763, ibid., 92.

21. Leopold Mozart to Lorenz Hagenauer, March 19, 1765, ibid., 184.

22. Eckermann, Gespräche mit Goethe, 390–91.

23. Leopold Mozart to Lorenz Hagenauer, April 25, 1764, Briefe, vol. 1, 146.

24. Leopold Mozart to Lorenz Hagenauer, February 1, 1764, ibid., 126.

25. Leopold Mozart to Lorenz Hagenauer, June 11, 1763, ibid., 69.

26. Leopold Mozart to Lorenz Hagenauer, August 20, 1763, ibid., 89.

27. Mozart to his sister, July 7, 1770, ibid., 369.

28. Leopold Mozart to Lorenz Hagenauer, January 30 and July 30, 1768, ibid., 256–57, 269–74, quotation at 272.

29. Leopold Mozart to his wife, April 3, 1770, ibid., 331.

30. Leopold Mozart to his wife, March 27, 1770, ibid., 327, 328.

31. Leopold Mozart to his wife, April 21, 1770, ibid., 338.

32. W. J. Turner, Mozart: The Man and His Works (1938; paperback ed. 1954), 85.

33. Leopold Mozart to his wife, May 19, 1770, Briefe, vol. 1, 348; Mozart to his sister, ibid., 350.

34. Mozart to his mother and sister, April 14, 1770, ibid., 336.

Chapter Two

1. Mozart to his father, December 20, 1777, Briefe, vol. 2, 199.

2. Mozart to his mother in Leopold Mozart to his wife, December 14, 1769, ibid., vol. 1, 292.

3. Leopold Mozart to his wife, November 17, 1770, ibid., 403.
4. Leopold Mozart to Maria Theresa Hagenauer, February 1, 1764, ibid., 121.
5. Solomon, Mozart, 38.
6. Leopold Mozart to his wife, May 8, 1770, Briefe, vol. 1, 407; to Lorenz Hagenauer, June 8, 1764, ibid., 154.
7. Leopold Mozart to Lorenz Hagenauer, March 19, 1765, ibid., 180–81.
8. Leopold Mozart to Lorenz Hagenauer, November 27, 1764, ibid., 173. Langegger also noted this inconsistency (Mozart, Vater und Sohn, 33).
9. Mozart to his sister in Leopold Mozart to his wife, December 30, 1774, Briefe, vol. 1, 513–14.
10. Leopold Mozart to his wife, December 29, 1770, ibid., 411.
11. H. C. Robbins Landon, "The Concertos: (2) Their Musical Origins and Development," Landon and Donald Mitchell, The Mozart Companion (1956), 248.
12. Mozart to his father, October 11, 1777, Briefe, vol. 2, 46.
13. Mozart to his sister, August 24, 1771, ibid., vol. 1, 432.
14. Mozart to his father, October 17, 1777, ibid., vol. 2, 66.
15. Solomon, Mozart, 163.
16. Ibid.
17. Mozart to Maria Anna Thekla Mozart, November 13, 1777, Briefe, vol. 2, 122–23.
18. Mozart to Maria Anna Thekla Mozart, November 5, 1777, ibid., 104.
19. Mozart to Maria Anna Thekla Mozart, November 5, 1777, ibid., 105.
20. Mozart to Maria Anna Thekla Mozart, November 13, 1777, ibid., 121.
21. Mozart to his father, February 22, 1778, ibid., 290.
22. Leopold Mozart to his son, February 12, 1778, ibid., 277–79.
23. Leopold Mozart to his son, December 11, 1777, ibid., 181–82.
24. Mozart to his father November 4, 1777, ibid., 101.
25. Mozart to his father, May 1, 1778, ibid., 343–45.
26. Mozart to his father, July 31, 1778, ibid., 427.
27. Mozart to his father, May 1, 1778, ibid., 345.
28. Mozart to his father, July 3, 1778, ibid., 388.
29. Ibid., 389.
30. Ibid.
31. Mozart to his father, July 31, 1778, ibid., 422.
32. Solomon (Mozart, 169) notes that, as the manuscript shows, this is what Nissen wrote, but the published version was far more decorous.

33. Mozart to Maria Anna Thekla Mozart, December 23, 1778, Briefe, vol. 2, 524.

Chapter Three

1. Solomon, Mozart, 99.
2. Charles Burney, The Present State of Music in Germany, the Netherlands, and the United Provinces (2nd ed., 1773), vol. 2, 322.
3. Mozart to his father, November 13, 1780, Briefe, vol. 3, 19.
4. Stanley Sadie, The New Grove Mozart (1983), 31.
5. Mozart to his father, September 30, 1777, Briefe, vol. 2, 23.
6. Mozart (really Leopold Mozart), mid-August 1777, ibid., 4–5.
7. Archishop of Salzburg to Mozart, Deutsch, Documentary Biography, 163.
8. Mozart to Abbé Bullinger, August 7, 1778, Briefe, vol. 2, 438.
9. Mozart to his father, September 11, 1778, ibid., 472–73.
10. Mozart to his father, October 15, 1778, ibid., 495–96.
11. Archbishop of Salzburg to Mozart, Deutsch, Documentary Biography, 182.
12. Mozart to his father, December 16, 1780, Briefe, vol. 3, 60.
13. Daniel Heartz, Mozart's Operas, ed. Thomas Baumann (1990), ch. 1, "Sacrifice Dramas."
14. Niemetschek, Leben, 21.
15. Quoted in Heartz, Mozart's Operas, 8n.
16. Mozart to his father, March 17, 1781, Briefe, vol. 3, 94–95.
17. Mozart to his father, May 12, 1781, ibid., 113.
18. See especially Mozart to his father, May 9 and 12, 1781, ibid., 111, 112.
19. Mozart to his father, May 12, 1781, ibid., 111.
20. Mozart to his father, May 16 and 19, 1781, ibid., 116, 118.
21. Mozart to his father, June 9, 1781, ibid., 127.
22. Mozart to his father, June 9, 1781, ibid., 126, 127.

Chapter Four

1. Nicholas Till, Mozart and the Enlightenment: Truth, Virtue and Beauty in Mozart's Operas (1992), 93.

2. Mozart to his father, March 24, 1781, Briefe, vol. 3, 99.

3. Mozart to his father, April 10, 1782, Briefe, vol. 3, 200.

4. Leopold Mozart to his son, December 11, 1780, ibid., 53.

5. Mozart to his father, April 10, 1782, ibid., 200. The word is "besoffen."

6. See Mozart to his father, December 15, 1781, ibid., 180.

7. Ibid., 181.

8. Ibid.

9. Ibid.

10. Mozart to his wife, May 23, 1789, ibid. vol. 4, 90.

11. Mozart to his father, February 14, 1778, ibid., vol. 2, 281.

12. Philip G. Downs, Classical Music: The Era of Haydn, Mozart, and Beethoven (1992), 488.

13. Sadie, New Grove Mozart, 93.

14. Quoted in Ernst Fritz Schmid, "Haydn and Mozart," The Creative World of Mozart, ed. Paul Henry Lang (1963), 99.

15. Leopold Mozart to his daughter, February 16, 1785, Briefe, vol. 3, 373.

16. Mozart to his father, April 10, 1784, ibid., 309.

17. Solomon, Mozart, 325.

18. Mozart to his father, May 21, 1783, Briefe, vol. 3, 270.

19. Leo Gershoy, From Despotism to Revolution, 1763–1789 (1944), 105.

Chapter Five

1. Mozart to Franz Anton Hoffmeister, November 20, 1785, Briefe, vol. 3, 454.

2. Mozart to his father, January 23, 1782, ibid., 195.

3. Solomon, Mozart, 297, 521–28.

4. Mozart to his father, August 22, 1781, Briefe, vol. 3, 151.

5. Leopold Mozart to his daughter, February 16, 1785, ibid., 372.

6. Solomon, Mozart, 298.

7. Niemetschek, Leben, 64.

8. Ibid., 34.

9. Mozart to his wife, September 30, 1790, Briefe, vol. 4, 114.

10. Mozart to Michael Puchberg, June 1788, ibid., 65.

11. Mozart to Michael Puchberg, June 17, 1788, ibid., 65–66.

12. Mozart to Michael Puchberg, July 12 and 14, 1789, ibid., 92–93.

13. Mozart to Michael Puchberg, July 17, 1789, ibid., 94–95.

14. Mozart to Michael Puchberg, end of March/beginning of April 1790, ibid., 104–105.
15. Leopold Mozart to his daughter, March 19, 1785, ibid., 380.
16. Mozart to his father, April 4, 1787, ibid., 41.
17. Mozart to Michael Puchberg, June 27, 1787, ibid., 69.

Chapter Six

1. Leopold Mozart to his daughter, November 28, 1785, Briefe, vol. 3, 905.
2. Walter Piston, Counterpoint (1947), 9.
3. Mozart to his father, April 20, 1782, Briefe, vol. 3, 202.
4. Mozart to his father, December 28, 1782, Briefe, vol. 3, 245–46.
5. Leopold Mozart to his daughter, February 16, 1785, ibid., 373.
6. Mozart to his father, October 31, 1783, ibid., 291.
7. For persuasive proof, see Alan Tyson, Mozart: Studies of the Autograph Scores (1987).
8. Mozart to his father, May 16, 1781, Briefe, vol. 3, 116; May 26, 1781, ibid., 120–21.
9. Ibid.
10. Sadie, New Grove Mozart, 116.
11. Charles Rosen, The Classical Style: Haydn, Mozart, Beethoven (1971, 2nd ed. 1976), 274.
12. Johann Abraham Peter Schulz, "Symphonie," in Johann Georg Sulzer, Allgemeine Theorie der schönen Künste, 4 vols. in 2 (1771–74). My attention was called to this dictionary entry by Elaine R. Sisman, Mozart: The "Jupiter" Symphony: No. 41 in C Major, K. 551 (1993), 9–10.
13. Alfred Einstein, Mozart: His Character, His Work, tr. Arthur Mendel and Nathan Broder (1945), 216.
14. Donald Francis Tovey, "Symphony in C Major (Köchel's Catalogue, No. 551)," Essays in Musical Analysis: Symphonies and Other Works (2nd ed., 1981), 443.
15. Quoted in Sisman, "Jupiter" Symphony, 29.
16. Downs, Classical Music, 521.
17. Konrad Küster, Mozart: Eine musikalische Biographie (1990; paperback ed. 1995), 327–28.

18. Downs, Classical Music, 521.

19. Wye J. Allanbrook, "Mozart's Tunes and the Comedy of Closure," On Mozart, ed. James M. Morris (1994), 185.

Chapter Seven

1. Mozart to his father, February 7, 1778, Briefe, vol. 2, 264.

2. Leopold Mozart to Lorenz Hagenauer, May 28, 1764, ibid., vol. 1, 152.

3. Mozart to his sister, October 26, 1771, ibid., 446–47.

4. Mozart to his father, October 11, 1777, ibid., vol. 2, 46.

5. Mozart to his father, February 4, 1778, ibid., 254.

6. Mozart to his father, October 13, 1781, ibid., vol. 3, 167. For a good treatment of this episode, see Gerald Abraham, "The Operas," The Mozart Companion, ed. H. C. Robbins Landon and Donald Mitchell (1956), 286–90.

7. Mozart to his father, May 7, 1783, Briefe, vol. 3, 268.

8. Mozart to his father, November 8, 13, 15, and 30, 1780, ibid., 13, 17, 20, 34–35.

9. Mozart to his father, January 18, 1783, ibid., 90.

10. Mozart to his father, May 7, 1781, ibid., 268.

11. Mozart to his father, July 5, 1783, ibid., 278.

12. Beaumarchais, Le Mariage de Figaro (1784), act 5, scene 3.

13. Theodor Billroth to Wilhelm Lübke, October 29, 1881, Briefe von Theodor Billroth (1895; 8th ed., 1910), 227.

14. Mozart to Gottfried von Jacquin, January 15, 1787, Briefe, vol. 4, 8.

15. Mozart to Gottfried von Jacquin, November 4, 1787, ibid., 58.

16. Edward J. Dent, Mozart's Operas: A Critical Study (1913; 2nd ed. 1947), 177.

17. Charles Gounod, Mozart's Don Giovanni: A Commentary (n.d.; tr. from 3rd ed. by Windeyer Clark, 1895), 1.

18. Deutsch, Documentary Biography, 313–15.

19. Dent, Mozart's Operas, 190; Joseph Kerman, Opera as Drama (1956; paperback ed. 1959), 109.

20. Dent, Mozart's Operas, 201.

21. G. B. Shaw, March 8, 1893, Music in London, 1890–94, 3 vols. (1932), vol. 2, 261.

Chapter Eight

1. Constanze Nissen to Abbé Maximilian Stadler, May 31, 1827, Briefe, vol. 4, 491.

2. Rosen, Classical Style, 368.

3. Küster, Mozart, 410.

4. Niemetschek, W. A. Mozart's Leben, 35.

5. Haydn to Michael Puchberg, January 1792, in Karl Geiringer, Haydn: A Creative Life in Music (1946; 2nd ed. 1963), 138.

6. Deutsch, Documentary Biography, 418–24.

7. Mozart to his wife, June 11, 1791, Briefe, vol. 4, 136.

8. Mozart to his wife, October 7, 8, and 14, 1791, ibid., 157, 162.

9. Mozart to his wife, July 7, 1791, ibid., 150.

10. Niemetschek, W. A. Mozart's Leben, 34.

11. See especially John M. Opitz, "Mozart's Sickness unto Death," unpublished paper for the symposium "Mozart in Montana – A Humanistic 200 Years' Commemoration" (1991); and Anton Neumayr, "Wolfgang Amadeus Mozart – Krankheit, Tod und Begräbnis," Genie und Alltag: Bürgerliche Stadtkultur zur Mozartzeit, ed. Gunda Barth-Scalmani, Brigitte Mazohl-Wallnig, Ernst Wangermann (1994), 119–33.

12. On this point, see the persuasive argument by Solomon, Mozart, 496–98.

13. Hector Berlioz, Mémoires, ed. Pierre Citron (1859; 1864; 1991), 107.

14. Felix Mendelssohn to Karl Friedrich Zelter, February 15, 1832, Mendelssohn: A Life in Letters, ed. Rudolf Elvers (1984), tr. Craig Tomlinson (1986), 178.

15. Maurice J. E. Brown, The New Grove Schubert (1980; rev. ed. 1982), 14.

16. Felix Weingartner, "Zurück zu Mozart!" (ca. 1910), Akkorde: Gesammelte Aufsätze (1912), quoted in Leon Botstein, "Nineteenth-Century Mozart: The Fin-de-siècle Mozart Revival," On Mozart, ed. James M. Morris (1994), 204.

17. Bruno Walter, Theme and Variations: An Autobiography, tr. James A. Galston (1966), 54.

BIBLIOGRAPHICAL NOTE

Mozart has been fortunate in his biographers. The first life, short and anecdotal, the source of some indispensable (and some imaginatively embroidered) stories is Franz Xaver Niemetschek, Leben des K. K. Kapellmeisters Wolfgang Gottlieb Mozart nach Originalquellen beschrieben (1798; 2nd ed. 1808), by one of Mozart's adorers from Prague. In contrast, the most recent full biography, Maynard Solomon's Mozart: A Life (1995), is impressive with its psychoanalytic perspective and its mastery of the musical material; beautifully detailed (more than six hundred pages, which include an invaluable estimate of Mozart's earnings year by year) and impressively researched, the book is as informative about Mozart's career as it is penetrating about his inner life. My biography, most notably in its handling of the endemic father-son conflict, is deeply indebted to Solomon's magisterial work. Florian Langegger, Mozart, Vater und Sohn: Eine psychologische Untersuchung (1978: 2nd ed. 1986) is disappointing.

Other lives deserving particular attention are Otto Jahn's justly celebrated, widely cited, and much exploited W. A.

Mozart, 2 vols. (1856; 4th ed. rev. Hermann Deiters, 1905–7; tr. Pauline D. Townsend, The Life of Mozart, 3 vols. [1882]); Théodore de Wyzewa and Georges de Saint-Foix, Wolfgang Amédé Mozart: Sa vie musicale et son oeuvre, 5 vols. (1912–46), especially valuable for its exhaustive analysis of Mozart's musical environment; and the thoughtful, suggestive study by Alfred Einstein, a major Mozart scholar, Mozart: His Character, His Work (tr. Arthur Mendel and Nathan Broder, 1945), which eschews chronology in favor of major themes. Mozart by Wolfgang Hildesheimer, essayist, short story writer, and translator, is ruminative (Solomon calls it "a loosely structured meditation") but offers, for all its idiosyncrasies, a subtle if controversial portrait. Two readable short lives are W. J. Turner, Mozart: The Man and His Works (1938), which uses Mozart's letters to advantage, and Stanley Sadie's neat and dependable The New Grove Mozart (1983), which has a convenient catalog of Mozart's works.

One subject of exceptional importance in the making and unmaking of legends about Mozart is the true history of his last illness and death. I have relied mainly on two persuasive analyses: Anton Neumayr, "Wolfgang Amadeus Mozart – Krankheit, Tod und Begräbnis," in Gunda Barth-Scalmani, Brigitte Mazohl-Wallnig, and Ernst Wangermann, eds., Genie und Alltag: Bürgerliche Stadtkultur zur Mozartzeit (1994), 119–33; and an unpublished paper by John M. Opitz, "Mozart's Sickness unto Death" (1991).

Mozart's life and work have been amply and accessibly documented. See Otto Erich Deutsch, ed., Mozart: Die Dokumente seines Lebens (1961) and Joseph Heinz Eibl, Addenda and Corrigenda (1978), together tr. Eric Blom,

Peter Branscombe, and Jeremy Noble, Mozart: A Documentary Biography (1965), very full but with some lacunae. No reproach can touch the critical edition of Mozart's correspondence (happily rounded out with letters from his father and others, and with satisfactory commentary): Wilhelm A. Bauer, Otto Erich Deutsch, and Joseph Heinz Eibl, eds., Mozart: Briefe und Aufzeichnungen, 7 vols. (1962–75), a veritable treasure trove from which I have freely drawn. Emily Anderson, ed. and tr., The Letters of Mozart and His Family, 3 vols. (3rd rev. ed., Stanley Sadie and Fiona Smart, 1985) is less definitive but precious to readers innocent of German.

The flood of special studies of Mozart's work and life continues unabated. (See the almost exhaustive bibliographies in Solomon [pp. 593–610] and Sadie [pp. 221–40].) I shall single out titles that made the most difference to me. The operas are astutely analyzed in Edward J. Dent, Mozart's Operas: A Critical Study (1913; 2nd ed. 1947), opinionated, a bit dated, but exceedingly worth reading. See also Daniel Heartz, ed. with contributing essays by Thomas Baumann, Mozart's Operas (1990), an elegant gathering of essays on such themes as "Donna Elvira and the Great Sextet" or "Coming of Age in Vienna: Die Entführung aus dem Serail." Brigid Brophy, Mozart the Dramatist: The Value of His Operas to Him, to His Age and to Us (1964; 2nd rev. ed. 1988) is a spirited and exhilarating polemic, presenting Mozart as a son of the Enlightenment. It may be read in conjunction with Nicholas Till's more detailed and scholarly Mozart and the Enlightenment: Truth, Virtue and Beauty in Mozart's Operas (1992), which takes the same tack. In this connection, the detective work by H. C. Robbins Landon in

Mozart and the Masons: New Light on the Lodge "Crowned Hope" (1982), an illustrated Walter Neurath Lecture, is of interest; so is Mozart and Masonry by Paul Nettl (1932; tr. Mrs. Robert Gold, 1957). See also Andrew Steptoe, The Mozart-DaPonte Operas: Cultural and Musical Background to Le nozze de Figaro, Don Giovanni, and Così fan tutte (1988).

Mozart's symphonies are explored by Georges de Saint-Foix, The Symphonies of Mozart (tr. Lesley Orrey, 1947); by Neal Zaslaw, Mozart's Symphonies: Context, Performance, Practice, Reception (1989); and by Elaine R. Sisman, Mozart: The "Jupiter" Symphony: No. 41 in C Major, K. 551 (1993) in a brief but meaty and suggestive monograph. For the quartets and the rest of his intimate music, greatly admired and always much played, there is above all A. Hyatt King, Mozart Chamber Music (1968; rev. ed. 1986). Probably the leading investigation of Mozart's marvelous keyboard music remains Cuthbert M. Girdlestone, Mozart's Piano Concertos (1939; tr. and enlarged, 1948), to be supplemented with Arthur Hutchings, A Companion to Mozart's Piano Concertos (1948; 2nd ed. 1958). In the course of a long and fertile career, Donald Francis Tovey wrote much splendid criticism of Mozart's music; his outstanding contribution to the study of Mozart's concertos is reprinted in Essays in Musical Analysis: Symphonies and Other Works, vol. 3 (1936), 3–46. For Mozart's unfinished and mysterious piece of church music, the Requiem, see especially Christoph Wolff, Mozart's Requiem: Historical and Analytical Studies, Documents, Score (1993). For Mozart's sacred music in general, the most informative study is R. G. Fellerer, Die Kirchenmusik W. A. Mozarts (1985). One highly specialized monograph, by Alan Tyson, Mozart: Studies of the Autograph Scores (1987), proves, among other things, that Mozart did not always equate his first with his final draft.

For Mozart the composer's world, Philip G. Downs's gratifyingly painstaking Classical Music: The Era of Haydn, Mozart, and Beethoven (1992) proves a helpful guide. In addition, we have the admirable long essays by Charles Rosen, which I read with great profit; they put Mozart (whose dark side he appreciates) into his musical context. See The Classical Style: Haydn, Mozart, Beethoven (1971; 2nd ed. 1976) and Sonata Form (1983). In his The Sonata in the Classic Era (1963), William S. Newman does not neglect Mozart. Mary Sue Morrow's beautifully informed Concert Life in Haydn's Vienna: Aspects of a Developing Musical and Social Institution (1989) throws clear light on the musical scene that Mozart came to know all too well. (It may be read with the first volume of the celebrated Viennese critic Eduard Hanslick's Geschichte des Concertwesens in Wien, 2 vols. [1869].) In this connection, two studies by H. C. Robbins Landon, Mozart: The Golden Years (1991) and 1791: Mozart's Last Year (1989), correct some persistent legends.

Of several collections of essays on Mozart, James M. Morris, ed., On Mozart (1994), is particularly rewarding. Among its most stimulating papers (to name only three) are William J. Baumol and Hilda Baumol, "On the Economics of Musical Composition in Mozart's Vienna" (pp. 72–101); Neal Zaslaw, "Mozart as a Working Stiff" (pp. 102–12); and Leon Botstein, "Nineteenth-Century Mozart: The Fin-de-siècle Mozart Revival" (pp. 204–26).

For Haydn, in addition to the major Mozart biographies

and the titles by Rosen, see the conventional and reliable biography by Karl Geiringer, Haydn: A Creative Life in Music (1946; 2nd ed. 1963). See also H. C. Robbins Landon, The Symphonies of Joseph Haydn (1955). Alexander Wheelock Thayer's brief Salieri: Rival of Mozart, which dates back to the mid-1860s, ed. Theodore Albrecht (1989), and April FitzLyon, Lorenzo da Ponte: A Biography of Mozart's Librettist (1955; complete ed. 1982) will have to do until more complete lives come along.

The better biographies describe Mozart's general environment – Salzburg, Vienna, mid-eighteenth-century Europe. Some essays in Genie und Alltag paint in the background. Notable are Brigitte Mazohl-Wallnig and Josef Wallnig on travel, "Reisen zur Mozart-Zeit – die Mozarts auf Reisen" (pp. 11–33); Mirko Herzog on clothing, " 'Wenn unsere Damen die Hausfrau an den Nagel hängen' ..." (35–101); and Werner Rainer on the social status of musicians, "Zum Sozialstatus des Berufsmusikers im 18. Jahrhundert am Beispiel der Salzburger Hofmusik" (243–58). For Prague, we have the charming chapter "Mozart in Prague" in Peter Demetz, Prague in Black and Gold: Scenes from the Life of a European City (1997). For Vienna, which still needs more rigorous treatment, see especially Ernst Wangermann, The Austrian Achievement, 1700–1800 (1973).

· LIVES · LIVES · LIVES · LI